Exercises for

When Words Collide

A Media Writer's Guide to Grammar and Style

Fourth Edition

Duncan McDonald
UNIVERSITY OF OREGON

Wadsworth Publishing Company
I(T)P™ An International Thomson Publishing Company

Belmont • Albany • Bonn • Boston • Cincinnati • Detroit • London • Madrid
Melbourne • Mexico City • New York • Paris • San Francisco • Singapore

COPYRIGHT © 1996 by Wadsworth Publishing Company
A Division of International Thomson Publishing Inc.
I(T)P   The ITP logo is a trademark under license.

Printed in the United States of America
1 2 3 4 5 6 7 8 9 10—01 00 99 98 97 96

For more information, contact Wadsworth Publishing Company.

Wadsworth Publishing Company
10 Davis Drive
Belmont, California 94002, USA

International Thomson Publishing Europe
Berkshire House 168-173
High Holborn
London, WC1V 7AA, England

Thomas Nelson Australia
102 Dodds Street
South Melbourne 3205
Victoria, Australia

Nelson Canada
1120 Birchmount Road
Scarborough, Ontario
Canada M1K 5G4

International Thomson Editores
Campos Eliseos 385, Piso 7
Col. Polanco
11560 México D.F. México

International Thomson Publishing GmbH
Königswinterer Strasse 418
53227 Bonn, Germany

International Thomson Publishing Asia
221 Henderson Road
#05-10 Henderson Building
Singapore 0315

International Thomson Publishing Japan
Hirakawacho Kyowa Building, 3F
2-2-1 Hirakawacho
Chiyoda-ku, Tokyo 102, Japan

ISBN 0-534-25741-0

Contents

	Introduction	1
	Pre-Exercise Review	2
EXERCISE 1	Diagnostic Test for Grammar, Punctuation and Spelling	12
EXERCISE 2	Parts of Speech 1	14
EXERCISE 3	Parts of Speech 2	17
EXERCISE 4	Parts of Speech 3	23
EXERCISE 5	Parts of Speech 4	25
EXERCISE 6	Identification of Sentence Elements	27
EXERCISE 7	Identification of Phrases and Clauses	32
EXERCISE 8	Creation of Phrases and Clauses	37
EXERCISE 9	Giving Power and Focus to Verbs	40
EXERCISE 10	Strengthening Modifiers	43
EXERCISE 11	Sentence Construction 1	45
EXERCISE 12	Sentence Construction 2	47
EXERCISE 13	Sentence Construction 3	49
EXERCISE 14	Subject-Verb Agreement	51
EXERCISE 15	Antecedent Agreement	53
EXERCISE 16	Case 1	55
EXERCISE 17	Case 2	57

EXERCISE 18   Parallel Structure   59

EXERCISE 19   Eliminating Sexism in Writing   61

EXERCISE 20   Proper Use Of Voice   63

EXERCISE 21   Restrictive and Non-Restrictive Constructions   65

EXERCISE 22   That/Which/Who and Restrictive/Non-Restrictive Constructions   67

EXERCISE 23   Punctuation 1   69

EXERCISE 24   Punctuation 2   71

EXERCISE 25   Punctuation 3   74

EXERCISE 26   Punctuation 4   76

EXERCISE 27   Subordination and Modification   78

EXERCISE 28   Word Use 1   80

EXERCISE 29   Word Use 2   82

EXERCISE 30   Word Use 3   84

EXERCISE 31   Spelling 1   86

EXERCISE 32   Spelling 2   87

EXERCISE 33   Spelling 3   88

EXERCISE 34   Spelling 4   90

EXERCISE 35   Editing for Grammar, Spelling and Style 1   91

EXERCISE 36   Editing for Grammar, Spelling and Style 2   93

EXERCISE 37   Clarity and Conciseness   95

EXERCISE 38   Boiling 1   98

EXERCISE 39   Boiling 2   99

EXERCISE 40   Final Grammar, Spelling and Word-Use Exam   100

Introduction

This set of exercises, which accompanies the fourth edition of *When Words Collide,* is more than a series of daunting tests.

It provides an opportunity to follow the *WWC* text closely and to improve methodically your understanding of grammar, style and structure. It allows you to work at your own pace, to return to material as needed and to heighten your confidence as a writer.

Your first use of this workbook should be completion of the Pre-Exercise Review (p.2). Note the answers and the page references to explanatory material. From there, you should work serially through all the testing material; you'll soon note that one "new building block" builds on one you have just completed.

As you move through these 40 exercises, we hope you will see the "blueprint" for the growth of your mastery of grammar and style. It parallels the organization of your *WWC* text, which you should use as a constant reference (that means friend) as you complete each exercise. Beginning with parts of speech and then moving through phrase and clause identification, sentence construction, agreement, case, voice, parallelism and spelling provides you with sense and order. Improving language skills is a tall order—and it's no time for anarchy and "free association"!

Finally, to prove that you really aren't alone and that education can be truly interactive, I want to offer some personal contact, which I know will benefit us both: Have a question? Want to argue about an answer? Want to discuss the delights (!) of grammar? Please pull onto the "InfoBahn" and send me an e-mail:

duncanm @ oregon.uoregon.edu

You will get a response, and it will be from me!

Good luck with your work—and remember that a judicious mix of curiosity and patience will always serve you well.

Duncan McDonald
University of Oregon

Pre-Exercise Review

The following 90 questions illustrate the range of material discussed in *When Words Collide* and examined in this exercise book. Before you start to tackle the 40 exercises in this book, please go over this review; examine each question and note the answer and, in many cases, the page references in the fourth edition of *When Words Collide*.

As you review this section, think not only of how your correct choices aid your understanding of the fundamentals of grammar, but of how this comprehension will help improve your writing as well.

1. Ollie feels sick that John won the lottery. What part of speech is *sick*? (A) *noun*, (B) *adjective*, (C) *adverb*.

   ANSWER: (B) *adjective. Sick* modifies the proper noun *Ollie*. The relationship between *sick* and *Ollie* is connected by the linking verb *feels*.

2. Rebuilding her country's shattered economy is her chief goal. What part of speech is *Rebuilding*? (A) *noun*, (B) *verb*, (C) *adjective*.

   ANSWER: (A) *noun*. Remember that *-ing* words aren't always verbs. They can be adjectives (participles) if they modify a noun, or they can be nouns (gerunds)—as in this case, when *Rebuilding* is the subject of the sentence.

3. This is the kind of allegation that hounds a person for years. What part of speech is *that*? (A) *conjunction*, (B) *noun*, (C) pronoun.

   ANSWER: (C) *pronoun. That* is called a *relative pronoun* because it relates to an antecedent in another part of a sentence (in this case, the noun *allegation*). *That* is the subject of the sentence's subordinate clause and depends on its antecedent to determine the number of its verb.

4. Before he shot the president, Hinckley reportedly spent several days (A) *laying* (B) *lying* around his hotel room.

   ANSWER: (B) *lying*. This verb is intransitive, which means it doesn't have a direct object. *Lay* requires a direct object; *lie* does not. Whereas *lay* means "to place," *lie* means "to recline."

5. The stock market continued its phenomenal rally today (A), (B); trading exceeded 20 million shares.

   ANSWER: (B); This sentence has two independent clauses. They can be separated by a comma only if they are joined by a coordinating conjunction (*and, but, or, nor, for yet,* or *so*). Without that conjunction, a semicolon is needed to create an abrupt break between these two complete thoughts.

6. *Acting on an anonymous phone call*, police today arrested prison escapee Harold Davis. The italicized sentence element is a (A) *verb,* (B) *subordinate clause,* (C) *participial phrase.*

   ANSWER: (C) *participial phrase.* The phrase acts as an adjective because it modifies the noun *police.* It is not a clause because it doesn't contain a subject and a verb.

7. He is a (A) *good natured* (B) *good-natured* (C) *good, natured* person.

   ANSWER: (B) *good-natured.* A compound modifier (in this case, an adjective modified by an adverb—both of which modify the noun *person*)—is hyphenated unless part of that modifier is an *-ly* adverb.

8. (A) *Your* (B) *You're* going to be very sorry if you eat that pickled tofu.

   ANSWER: (B) *You're. Your* is a possessive pronoun, not a contraction of *you* and *are.*

9. Harmonicas, (A) *that* (B) *which* are simple to play, are great companions when you're stuck in Toledo.

   ANSWER: (B) *which.* The commas are your clue that some non-essential material has been set inside the main clause. The clause *which are simple to play* is not necessary to the meaning of the sentence; therefore, the relative pronoun *that* is not used.

10. The woman (A) *who* (B) *whom* detectives believed committed the robbery has been cleared.

    ANSWER: (A) *who. You* should separate and reconstruct the two clauses to analyze this answer. The independent clause is *The woman has been cleared.* The dependent clause, reconstructed, is *who committed the robbery, detectives believed.* The pronoun of choice, then, is *who* because it is the subject of *committed.*

11. She had a hard time accepting (A) *him* (B) *his* eating cold pizza for breakfast.

    ANSWER: (B) *his.* The personal pronoun *him* is in the objective case. However, the possessive pronoun *his* is needed here because it modifies the noun (gerund) *eating.*

12. None of his clothes (A) *is* (B) *are* likely to fetch more than 50 cents at a rummage sale.

    ANSWER: (B) *are.* This is one of those rare cases in which *none* takes a plural verb. In this sentence, you could not say "not one of his clothes *is.*" Instead, *none* here means "not any of his clothes *are.*"

13. Many people don't support the (A) *press'* (B) *press's* stance in the school board recall.

    ANSWER: (A) *press'.* Remember this rule: If a singular common noun ends in *s* and the next word begins with *s*, add only an apostrophe to form the possessive.

14. Rick always remembered this: (A) *The* (B) *the* fundamental things apply as time goes by.

    ANSWER: (A) *The.* When a complete sentence follows a colon, its first letter is capitalized.

15. He called for his brother, for whom he had been searching all day (A) *,* (B) *;* but all he heard was the distant wail of a timber wolf.

    ANSWER: (B) *;* This is a compound-complex sentence (it has one dependent and two independent clauses). It also has internal punctuation before the needed semicolon. Such a sentence needs a more definite pause between thoughts, which a semicolon can provide.

16. (A) "*Is* (B) "*It's* just a matter of time until we can put together a winning season," the embattled athletic director told a quiet meeting of the alumni association.

    ANSWER: (B) *It's*. The athletic director is saying "It *is* just a matter of time." A contraction is needed, not the possessive *its*.

17. The criteria for judging the art contest (A) *was* (B) *were* never announced to the press.

    ANSWER: (B) *were*. *Criteria* is the plural of *criterion*. Watch for unusual and foreign plurals when determining the number of the verb.

18. Three million board feet of California redwood (A) *was* (B) *were* exported last month.

    ANSWER: (A) *was*. Although *feet* is a plural word, it has the meaning of a collective unit in this sentence. We get the sense of a large amount, not of many thousands of trees being shipped overseas. The intended meaning of a plural-sounding word may sometimes be singular.

19. The man (A) *who* (B) *whom* police arrested has confessed to the robbery.

    ANSWER: (B) *whom*. *Whom* is receiving the action of the clause, *police arrested whom*. It must be in the objective case. The main clause is. *The man has confessed to the robbery.*

20. Baseball is one of those games that (A) *don't require* (B) *doesn't require* extensive knowledge of rules to be enjoyed.

    ANSWER: (A) *don't require*. The correct antecedent of the relative pronoun *that* is *games*, not *one*. There are several games that obviously don't require extensive knowledge of rules, if we understand the meaning of the sentence. The meaning would be different, of course, if the writer meant to say that baseball is *the only one* of the games that *requires* a good understanding of rules.

21. Neither the city councillors nor the mayor (A) *has* (B) *have* been linked to the concession contract scandal.

    ANSWER: (A) *has*. When a compound subject (*councillors-mayor*) is in a *neither … nor/either … or* construction—or is separated by *but* or *or*—the part of the subject closest to the verb determines the number of the verb.

22. During the Great Depression, approximately two-thirds of the workforce (A) *was* (B) *were* employed.

    ANSWER: (A) *was*. When a word such as *half, plenty* or an actual fraction is the subject, the verb draws its number from the number of the prepositional phrase that follows the fraction. This, too, would be correct:

    One-third of employable workers <u>were</u> without jobs during the Great Depression.

23. Rains in the Midwest have delayed spring planting (A) , (B) ; however, sunny skies are forecast for the rest of the week.

    ANSWER: (B) ; When two independent clauses are not joined by coordinating conjunction such as *or, but* or *and*, a semicolon is needed. The conjunctive adverb *however* is not strong enough to pull those two clauses together with a mere comma.

24. There is no better soccer player on the squad than (A) *she* (B) *her*.

    ANSWER: (B) *her*. In this sentence, *than* is a preposition, not a conjunction of comparison. There is no implied comparison. You can't tack another clause ("than *she* is a soccer player") onto this sentence and have it make sense.

25. (A) *Whose* (B) *Who's* in charge here?

    ANSWER: (B) *Who's*. The possessive *whose* doesn't modify anything in this sentence. The contraction of *Who is—Who's—*is needed here to provide subject and verb.

26. She is a (A) *widely-traveled* (B) *widely traveled* anthropologist.

    ANSWER: (B) *widely traveled*. A compound modifier that has an *-ly* adverb in it does not require hyphenation.

27. Between you and (A) *me*, (B) *I*, the city's bond issue doesn't have a prayer at the polls.

    ANSWER: (A) *me*. As the object of the preposition *between*, the pronoun must be in the objective case.

28. There (A) *was* (B) *were* some years when farmers lost money and had to borrow from the bank.

    ANSWER: (B) *were*. *There*, an expletive, is not the subject of this sentence. In *there* constructions the true subject is usually preceded by the verb. In this sentence *years* is the subject and calls for a plural verb.

29. The agents are sworn to protect (A) *whoever* (B) *whomever* is elected to the office.

    ANSWER: (A) *whoever*. This pronoun is the subject of the clause *whoever is elected to the office* and must be in the nominative case.

30. The president's speech was well-orchestrated, but not many senators were swayed by (A) *him* (B) *it*.

    ANSWER: (B) *it*. The correct antecedent is *speech*. The possessive, *president's*, also modifies *speech*.

31. The news media (A) *is* (B) *are* not to blame for the current wave of doomsday attitudes.

    ANSWER: (B) *are*. *Media* (the word) is the plural of *medium*. It normally takes a plural verb.

32. The number of bank failures (A) *has* (B) *have* increased this year.

    ANSWER: (A) *has*. *The number* as a subject always takes a singular verb because its meaning is definite. *A number*, however, seems *less* specific and takes a plural verb.

33. Can you sit through "Gone with the (A) *Wind?*" (B) *Wind*"?

    ANSWER: (B) *Wind*"? Question marks go inside quotation marks only if the quoted material is a question. Example:

    The witness asked, "Do you expect me to jeopardize the life of my <u>brother?"</u>

34. None of her answers (A) *was* (B) *were* satisfactory.

    ANSWER: (A) *was*. The indefinite pronoun *none is* a real troublemaker because it takes either a singular or a plural verb according to the meaning of the sentence. In this example, *none* means that "no one answer" was satisfactory. However, in "The master chef said that none of the pan juices were satisfactory," you can't read "no one pan juice." So the rule of "no amount" comes into play. If you can read "no amount" into a *none* construction, the verb should be plural. On occasion, a sentence may seem right with either the singular or the plural verb; in that case, either stay with the singular or try to rewrite the sentence.

35. Focus the image, set the aperture and (A) *the shutter will trip when you press the button.* (B) *release the shutter by* pressing the button.

    ANSWER: *(B) release the shutter....* To maintain parallel structure in this sentence, keep the verb tense consistent. There is no reason to switch to the future tense here. The switch creates a break that disturbs the reader. Remember that consistency and clarity go hand in hand.

36. The (A) *warm northwest wind* (B) *warm, northwest wind* chased the Arctic chill that had gripped the area for two weeks.

    ANSWER: (A) *warm northwest wind*. A comma is not needed between *warm* and *northwest* because they are not separate modifiers. You cannot call it a warm *and* northwest wind (substituting *and* is a technique for determining whether a comma is needed between modifiers). Actually, *warm* modifies the term *northwest wind*. A *warm, gentle breeze is* properly punctuated because *warm* and *gentle* separately modify *breeze*.

37. I can tell you are not (A) *averse* (B) *adverse to* constructive criticism.

    ANSWER: (A) *averse*. It refers to a person's opposition or reluctance. *Adverse,* meaning "unfavorable or hostile," relates to things or concepts but never to people.

38. What (A) *affect* (B) *effect* do you think this will have on the team?

    ANSWER: (B) *effect*. A *noun* is needed here to describe a result. *Affect* is almost always a *verb*.

39. I don't appreciate your attempts to (A) *allude* (B) *elude* to my criminal past.

    ANSWER: (A) *allude*. An "indirect reference" is being made. *Elude* means "to escape."

40. Talks have resumed (A) *between* (B) *among* representatives of Argentina, Great Britain, the U.S. State Department and the United Nations.

    ANSWER: (A) *between*. There is a *direct* relationship between the parties, even though there are more than two. *Among* is better used when the meaning "distribution" is intended.

41. A number of economic advisers (A) *has* (B) *have* abandoned the administration recently.

    ANSWER: (B) *have*. *A number of* always takes a plural verb. If the article had been *the*, it would have taken a singular verb.

42. She is (A) *anxious* (B) *eager* to present her findings.

    ANSWER: (B) *eager.* Because she is excited at the prospect of doing this, she is *eager.* If she were suffering from fear or anxiety, she would be *anxious.* You are eager *to do* something but anxious *about* something.

43. The aircraft spun dizzily toward the ground (A) *as if* (B) *like* it had been slapped by a giant hand.

    ANSWER: (A) *as if.* It is a conjunction that introduces a clause, such as "it had been slapped." *Like* is used only as a preposition. It cannot introduce a clause.

44. Why did you select Susan for the committee rather than (A) *I* (B) *me?*

    ANSWER: (B) *me.* If a comparison is being made, you use the nominative case ("Do you think Tom is as sensitive as I?"). But the meaning halts at the preposition *than* in this sentence. It requires a simple *object*—in the objective case. One test is to try to carry out the thought implied in the sentence. If you can expand the sentence, it probably requires the nominative case.

    Do you think Tom is as sensitive as I? (am sensitive?)

    Why did you select Susan for the committee rather than (I was selected?) (*Me* is needed here.)

45. Tom feels (A) *bad* (B) *badly* about his team's loss.

    ANSWER: (A) *bad. We* are describing Tom's state in this linking verb construction. For example, we would not say "Tom feels sadly." An adjective, not an adverb, is called for.

46. His nightmares were (A) *because of* (B) *due to* his anxiety about his promotion.

    ANSWER: (B) *due to. You* can't answer the question *why* in this construction. That's the main cue for using *due to.* In addition, the linking verb *were* needs an adjective to relate to nightmares. *Because of,* a preposition, doesn't fit the bill.

47. Dispatches from the fighting in the Mideast have been (A) *censored* (B) *censured* by government officials.

    ANSWER: (A) *censored.* This information is being screened and edited, not condemned. People can be *censured* for their actions.

48. The speeding car (A) *collided with* (B) *crashed into* the telephone pole.

    ANSWER: (B) *crashed into.* Both objects have to be moving in order to *collide.*

49. Fifty-six people died on the state's highways this Memorial Day, (A) *compared to* (B) *compared with* last year's count of 49.

    ANSWER: (B) *compared with.* When you are making a side-by-side comparison to see similarities and differences, use *compared with. Compared to* means "likened to."

50. The mayor's stubbornness can be (A) *compared to* (B) *compared with* the dead-set stance of a brick wall.

    ANSWER: (A) *compared to.* In this sense, we are saying that the mayor's stubbornness can be "likened to" a brick wall. You can see that actual comparisons call for *compared with.*

51. Her success plan is (A) *composed of* (B) *comprised of* seven easy-to-learn steps.

    ANSWER: (A) *composed of.* To begin with, *comprised of is* a redundant phrase. When *comprise* alone is used, it means "include." A more direct way to write this example is, "Her success plan *comprises* seven steps." When you want to say "is made up of," choose *composed of.*

52. A (A) *continual* (B) *continuous* line of camels was silhouetted against the Saharan dusk.

    ANSWER: (B) *continuous.* A continuous line is "unbroken." *Continual* means "repeated or intermittent":

    Are your <u>continual</u> visits to the chiropractor really necessary?

    Some stylists argue that the distinctions between *continuous* and *continual* are now blurred. We believe there are meanings here to be preserved.

53. I have been (A) *persuaded* (B) *convinced* that I must change my vote on this issue.

    ANSWER: (A) *persuaded.* You receive persuasion; personal conviction is a state. You could say that you *are convinced* that a course of action is correct, but you could not *be convinced to* follow one.

54. Smith has always (A) *differed from* (B) *differed with* Taylor in temperament.

    ANSWER: (A) *dfffered from.* Smith is not disagreeing with Taylor; these two people are merely unlike or dissimilar in temperament. Use *differ with* only to show argument or debate.

55. The (A) *enormity* (B) *enormousness* of the Mount Everest expedition has staggered even the most organized and experienced climbers.

    ANSWER: (B) *enormousness.* We are talking about size—in this case, huge proportions. *Enormity* means "wickedness."

56. The forlorn-looking group moved (A) *further* (B) *farther* down the road.

    ANSWER: (B) *farther.* We are discussing distance, not degree. There may *seem* to be distance associated with *further,* but it is more conceptual than concrete.

    The planning subcommittee said it will study the recommendation <u>further.</u>

57. The candidate said this country needs (A) *fewer* (B) *less* welfare programs and more work-incentive projects.

    ANSWER: (A) *fewer.* If you can get the sense of "specific or identifiable numbers," use *fewer.* Use *less* when you are talking about "amounts, quantity, sums and concepts." The following example shows this difference:

    This country needs <u>fewer politicians</u> and <u>less politics.</u>

58. O'Shea reportedly (A) *hanged* (B) *hung* himself in his jail cell rather than face his embezzlement trial.

    ANSWER: (A) *Hanged.* People *hang* themselves. Whether it is by their own hand or by others', they are *hanged.* Pictures and other inanimate objects are *hung.* However, if O'Shea had been dead for several hours before his body was discovered, it would bc correct to write that his body '"*hung* in the cell for several hours."

59. Are you (A) *implying* (B) *inferring* that the treasurer's report is false?

    ANSWER: (A) *implying.* What is being questioned is "a hint or suggestion that apparently is being made." You can *infer* something ("make a deduction") from someone's implication. Think of *implying* as more direct and aggressive (as in "making a charge or accusation") and of *inferring* as more passive and contemplative ("figuring out what was meant by the implication").

60. The winning highway bid was (A) *less than* (B) *under* $45 million.

    ANSWER: (A) *less than.* Use *under* only if something is physically, rather than figuratively, under something else.

    He was pinned <u>under</u> the wheels of the jackknifed trailer.

    Less than always refers to "quantity or amount."

61. (A) *More than* (B) *Over* 5,000 demonstrators clogged downtown streets to protest the arrival of the nuclear submarine.

    ANSWER: (A) *More than.* Use the same logic as in the previous answer. Planes fly *over* mountains, but a budgeted figure is *more than* $2 million.

62. The four-car accident (A) *occurred* (B) *took place* on a foggy section of Interstate 405 near Tigard.

    ANSWER: (A) *occurred.* Use *take place* only to refer to something that has been scheduled.

63. Only 12 (A) *people* (B) *persons* attended the school budget meeting.

    ANSWER: (A) *people.* In the case of *person,* two's a crowd. If you have more than one person, you have *people.* It's a simple rule that will help you avoid unnecessarily complicated decisions.

64. His (A) *principals* (B) *principles* yielded like the skin of a rotten apple when he was offered fame and fortune.

    ANSWER: (B) *principles.* As the subject of the sentence, *principles* is a noun. *Principals* in this case would have meant "someone in authority," such as a school principal. But this sentence refers to "beliefs and rules of conduct"—*principles*—which can only be a noun. *Principal* can also be an adjective when it means "main or chief," as in "the *principal* reason for denying the petition."

65. In the opinion of courthouse regulars, the prosecution has not (A) *proved* (B) *proven* that Robinson is an arsonist.

    ANSWER: (A) *proved.* The preferred past and past perfect form of the verb *prove* is *proved.* However, *proven* can be used as an adjective, as in "something can be proven." (*Proven* modifies *something.*) As far as this sentence is concerned, if the prosecution has not *proved* guilt, then the defendant is not a *proven* arsonist.

66. (A) *Because* (B) *Since* the state is far behind in revenue collections, the governor will ask the legislate to convene.

    ANSWER: (A) *Because. Since* should be used only to denote "a period of time."

    The city has offered free parking <u>since</u> 1945.

    Use *because* to indicate "a reason or cause."

67. The smell of gardenias invariably (A) *evokes* (B) *invokes* memories of the funeral.

    ANSWER: (A) *evokes.* In this sentence, the gardenias are helping to "recall" memories of the funeral. To *invoke* would be to "call upon" or to "implore":

    Athena <u>invoked</u> the power of the gods to help her retain her beauty.

68. She promised to (A) *lend* (B) *loan* me her car while mine was being repaired.

    ANSWER: (A) *lend.* You can't go wrong using *lend* in all situations as a verb meaning "allow to borrow." However, loan is used as a verb in the context of a financial transaction:

    The bank refused to <u>loan</u> him sufficient funds for the project.

    Loan is generally a noun.

69. The goal of her Midwest whistle-stop tour was to (A) *elicit* (B) *illicit* $5 million in campaign funds.

    ANSWER: (A) *elicit.* To *elicit* means "to draw forth" or "gather." *Illicit* is an adjective, not a verb. It means "improper or illegal."

70. An internationally (A) *renown* (B) *renowned* photojournalist, he is equally (A) *renown* (B) *renowned* for his arrogance.

    ANSWER: (B) *renowned*—for both. *Renown* is a noun, as in "She is a writer of great *renown.*"

71. The general called the Persian Gulf invasion an (A) *historic* (B) *historical* moment.

    ANSWER: (A) *historic.* In this context, the meaning relates to an important moment in history. It is not *about* history.

72. The president's proposed budget (A) *constitutes* (B) *comprises* (C) *is comprised* of three new domestic spending plans.

    ANSWER: (B) *comprises.* When *you* realize that *comprises* means "includes," you understand that "is comprised of" is *never* correct usage. A whole (budget) comprises (includes) its parts (plans). The parts *constitute* the whole.

73. I'll do everything I can to (A) *ensure* (B) *insure* the acceptance of your credentials at the convention.

    ANSWER: (A) *ensure.* Remember that *insure* is used only in an actual insurance context. If you want to guarantee something besides insurance coverage, use *ensure.*

74. Jensen is a strong *advocate* of government-subsidized health insurance. What part of speech is *advocate?* (A) *direct object,* (B) *pronoun,* (c) *appositive,* (D) *predicate nominative.*

    ANSWER: (D) *predicate nominative.* The linking verb *is* gives an important clue—it links the noun *advocate* to *Jensen.*

75. He is one of those chefs *who* never reveal recipes. What part of speech is *who?* (A) *conjunction,* (B) *relative pronoun,* (C) *personal pronoun,* (D) *antecedent.*

    ANSWER: (B) *relative pronoun.* As a noun substitute, the relative pronoun *who* refers (relates) to the noun *chefs;* in doing so, it controls the number of the verb, the plural *reveal.*

Note: Answers for the last questions are at the end of this section. Look at each group of four words, and identify the misspelled word, if any. If you think a word is *misspelled,* spell it correctly. If you think that all words are *correct,* go to the next group.

76. desirable exuseable irresistible noticeable
77. leisure hygiene yield weird
78. relevant persistant resistant superintendent
79. accumulate separate accomodate appropriate
80. cancelled omitted traveled committed
81. proceed accede precede supersede
82. dilemma broccoli innoculate vilify
83. protein harrassment recommend questionnaire
84. batallion medallion sacrilegious financier
85. judgement commitment occasion ecstasy
86. believe discernable withhold conscious
87. desperate pretentious concensus embarrass
88. definately incidence occurrence phenomenal
89. wield existance maintenance superficial
90. activate omission perceptible enforceable

ANSWERS:

76. excusable
77. all are correct
78. persistent
79. accommodate
80. canceled
81. all are correct
82. inoculate
83. harassment
84. battalion
85. judgment
86. discernible
87. consensus
88. definitely
89. existence
90. all are correct

EXERCISE 1

Diagnostic Test for Grammar, Punctuation and Spelling

Purpose: To identify levels of competency and areas of weakness in grammar, punctuation and spelling.

Instructions: Select the correct choice in each of the following sentences. To help you properly assess your current level of expertise, please do not use any reference aids.

GRAMMAR AND PUNCTUATION

_____ 1. The construction "While England slept" is called a **(a) clause (b) phrase**.

_____ 2. In the sentence "Newt fired the entire congressional staff," the word *entire* is called an **(a) adverb (b) adjective**.

_____ 3. The sentence "She slept through the night" contains a/an **(a) linking (b) transitive (c) intransitive** verb.

_____ 4. Yes, this is one of those diagnostic tests **(a) which (b) that** drives students crazy.

_____ 5. None of the women had **(a) her (b) their** assessment reduced.

_____ 6. Neither of the tax measures **(a) has (b) have** failed.

_____ 7. She finished her letter with the sign-off, "I remain **(a) yours (b) your's** truly."

_____ 8. **(a) Who's (b) Whose** book is this?

_____ 9. **(a) Who's (b) Whose** in charge here?

_____ 10. The college is deeply interested in **(a) it's (b) its (c) their** alumni.

_____ 11. In the sentence "Building an empire is not an overnight project," the word building is a/an **(a) verb (b) infinitive (c) gerund (d) predicate**.

_____ 12. She is one of those writers who never **(a) miss (b) misses** a deadline.

_____ 13. Among the recently unearthed treasures from the trouble-ridden dig **(a) is (b) are** a string of 10,000-year-old pearls.

_____ 14. Frank feels **(a) bad (b) badly** about not making it to the finals of the Mansfield Muskrat-Calling Contest.

_____ 15. It looks **(a) like (b) as if** the referendum will fail.

_____ 16. He took the job **(a) , because (b) because** he needed the money.

_____ 17. Is this woeful wombat **(a) your's (b) yours**?

_____ 18. You know very well that she is far more intelligent than **(a) I (b) me**.

_____ 19. The senator announced that she "would not run **(a) again". (b) again."**

_____ 20. You will never find a better editor than **(a) he (b) him**.

_____ 21. Yes, it was **(a) she (b) her** who started the company.

_____ 22. The computer, along with all its peripherals, **(a) retail (b) retails** for only $1,500.

_____ 23. She is an **(a) internationally-acclaimed (b) internationally acclaimed** cellist.

_____ 24. I really don't want to argue the point with you **(a), but (b); but** you're absolutely wrong about that movie!

_____ 25. I don't believe you've **(a) proved (b) proven** your point.

_____ 26. He **(a) lay (b) laid** on the couch, crying deep into the night.

_____ 27. The lonely lamprey **(a) said (b) said, (c) said:** "You picked a fine time to leave me, you eel."

_____ 28. The blue chip stocks managed a modest gain **(a) , (b) ; (c):** the bond market dropped sharply.

_____ 29. I think that **(a) we (b) us** freelancers ought to unionize.

_____ 30. The new treasurer said she is **(a) eager (b) anxious** to take office.

_____ 31. It looks **(a) like (b) as if** it will rain tonight.

_____ 32. Creating new investment opportunities **(a) has (b) have** made her a legend on Wall Street.

_____ 33. The bus **(a) that (b) which** stops at this corner is on an express line.

_____ 34. He lectured about the perils of smoking to **(a) whoever (b) whomever** would listen.

_____ 35. This is the person **(a) who (b) whom** police suspect of the crime.

SPELLING

Instructions: Please choose the _misspelled_ word from each group of three words and put your letter selection in the space provided. Alternate or secondary listings in a dictionary are _not_ considered correct in this exercise.

_____ 36. a. weird	b. wield	c. seige
_____ 37. a. judgment	b. concensus	c. excusable
_____ 38. a. grievous	b. harrassment	c. heinous
_____ 39. a. accumulate	b. accelerate	c. accomodate
_____ 40. a. procede	b. precede	c. precedence
_____ 41. a. travelled	b. canceled	c. committed
_____ 42. a. batallion	b. medallion	c. balloon
_____ 43. a. occassion	b. vacillate	c. occurred
_____ 44. a. seperate	b. deceive	c. credible
_____ 45. a. mathematics	b. atheletics	c. parallel
_____ 46. a. physician	b. chancellor	c. sherriff
_____ 47. a. forty	b. fiery	c. fullfill
_____ 48. a. antecendent	b. relevant	c. superintendant
_____ 49. a. recommend	b. recieve	c. retention
_____ 50. a. lonliness	b. likable	c. irretrievable

EXERCISE 2

Parts of Speech 1

Purpose: To sharpen skills in identifying the verb, the "drive train" of the sentence; to distinguish verbs from verbals.

Reference: *WWC* (4/e), pp. 11-19

VERBS

Instructions: In items 1-15, please circle the verb in each sentence. In the space provided, indicate whether the verb is transitive (T), intransitive (I) or linking (L).

Example:

___I___ The bank (foreclosed) on the mortgage.

_____ 1. He wants the pasta special with prawns.

_____ 2. She wants to dream the impossible dream.

_____ 3. Why do fools fall in love?

_____ 4. Are you well today?

_____ 5. Are you feeling better today?

_____ 6. This cranberry quiche tastes terrible!

_____ 7. Speaking extemporaneously, she destroyed her opponent's arguments.

_____ 8. Please lay the book here.

_____ 9. Please lay down for a few minutes.

_____ 10. Whom will you invite to the party?

_____ 11. His legacy will continue through the family's endowment.

_____ 12. The border guard accepted the bribe.

_____ 13. Tom feels bad about his engineering the protest march.

_____ 14. Samantha left hurriedly.

_____ 15. What exactly do you want?

VERBALS

Instructions: For sentences 16-25, please circle the verbal in each sentence and indicate in the space provided whether it is an Infinitive (I), a Gerund (G) or a Participle (P).

Example:

___G___ (Building) bridges is his specialty.

_____ 16. Traveling unaccompanied through Tanzanian bush country, he was constantly on the lookout for ivory poachers.

_____ 17. Do you know how to build a nest for the Crimson-Waxed Hornbill?

_____ 18. She eats sensibly, hoping that her cholesterol one day will drop to normal levels.

_____ 19. The blinding, driving snow sent drivers sliding off the roadway.

_____ 20. He enjoys painting conservative slogans on recently renovated housing projects.

_____ 21. I will never understand why you chose to join the Tofu Liberation Army.

_____ 22. Researching the effects of televised violence on preteens is her academic specialty.

_____ 23. The hard-hitting series in the Philadelphia Inquirer was influential enough to prompt a congressional investigation.

_____ 24. I'll never understand why you persisted in complaining about the wilted cabbage!

_____ 25. Flanked by her codefendants, she marched resolutely into the courtroom.

USING VERBS AND VERBALS

Instructions: For items 26-35, please write *two* sentences using each of the verb forms listed below. First, create a sentence using that *verb* in the *past tense*; then write a second sentence that uses the verb form to create either a gerund, participial phrase or infinitive.

Example:

Win

(Verb, past tense): She *won* the javelin event.

(Gerund): *Winning* is a great revenge.

26. Lecture

_____

_____

27. Complete

_____

_____

28. Swing

_____

_____

29. Plead

_____

_____

30. Drive

_____

_____

31. Drag

_____

_____

32. Cook

_____

_____

33. Lead

_____

_____

34. Address

_____

_____

35. Cultivate

_____

_____

EXERCISE 3

Parts of Speech 2

Purpose: To build recognition of all parts of speech as the foundation for grammatical principles and sentence construction.

Reference: *WWC* (4/e), Chapter 2

Instructions: Identify the italicized part of speech in the following sentences from the choices offered.

_____ 1. You should be proud of your *efforts*.
   a. noun
   b. verb
   c. adjective
   d. pronoun

_____ 2. Your *bravery* in the face of such conflict truly amazes me.
   a. adverb
   b. noun
   c. adjective
   d. verb

_____ 3. Do you remember a television show called *"Mr. Peepers"*?
   a. interjection
   b. verb
   c. pronoun
   d. noun

_____ 4. Why, it's Megan *herself*!
   a. noun
   b. pronoun
   c. adjective
   d. adverb

_____ 5. The suspect barricaded himself *inside* the house.
   a. adverb
   b. conjunction
   c. preposition
   d. verb

_____ 6. Statutes such as *this* give judges nightmares.
   a. noun
   b. adjective
   c. pronoun
   d. adverb

_____ 7. The revelation is *damaging* to her case.
   a. verb
   b. adjective
   c. noun
   d. adverb

_____ 8. *Neither* of your conditions is acceptable.
   a. interjection
   b. conjunction
   c. noun
   d. pronoun

_____ 9. *While* I lay sleeping, someone stole my tea cozy.
   a. adverb
   b. conjunction
   c. preposition
   d. noun

_____ 10. It looks *as if* the drought will end soon.
   a. conjunction
   b. preposition
   c. adverb
   d. verb

_____ 11. *Flooding* that compartment is the only way to contain the fire.
   a. noun
   b. verb
   c. adverb
   d. conjunction

_____ 12. The opening ceremonies should begin *shortly*.
   a. adjective
   b. preposition
   c. adverb
   d. verb

_____ 13. Councillors approved the ordinance *but* defeated the budget resolution.
    a. verb
    b. preposition
    c. adverb
    d. conjunction

_____ 14. *Continuing* its historic rally, the stock market today gained 40 more points.
    a. conjunction
    b. verb
    c. adjective
    d. adverb

_____ 15. Our agency has no better advertising copywriter *than* her.
    a. pronoun
    b. preposition
    c. conjunction
    d. adverb

_____ 16. Please place the wombat *here* on the couch.
    a. adverb
    b. preposition
    c. pronoun
    d. adjective

_____ 17. Do you feel *well* today?
    a. adverb
    b. adjective
    c. conjunction
    d. pronoun

_____ 18. She writes *well*, don't you agree?
    a. adverb
    b. adjective
    c. conjunction
    d. pronoun

_____ 19. La Crosse is a city in western *Wisconsin*.
    a. pronoun
    b. noun
    c. interjection
    d. adjective

_____ 20. I don't *appreciate* your patronizing tone.
  a. adjective
  b. adverb
  c. noun
  d. verb

_____ 21. *Now* it can be told!
  a. adverb
  b. preposition
  c. adjective
  d. pronoun

_____ 22. This is one of those sentences *that* give students ulcers.
  a. pronoun
  b. preposition
  c. conjunction
  d. adverb

_____ 23. Reviewers called her production "the *most* stunning cinematic feat at the festival."
  a. adjective
  b. conjunction
  c. adverb
  d. preposition

_____ 24. The union refuses to sign the contract *because* the pension provisions don't contain a cost-of-living clause.
  a. adverb
  b. preposition
  c. conjunction
  d. pronoun

_____ 25. *Because of* your recalcitrance, you're not going to be assigned to the San Diego bureau.
  a. adverb
  b. preposition
  c. conjunction
  d. pronoun

_____ 26. *Ouch*! That really hurt!
  a. verb
  b. adverb
  c. interjection
  d. preposition

_____ 27. The team continues *its* phenomenal rally.
  a. verb contraction
  b. noun
  c. adjective
  d. pronoun

_____ 28. *Blinding* snow has closed highways in three Midwesten states.
  a. noun
  b. adjective
  c. verb
  d. adverb

_____ 29. Neither the nuclear freeze ordinance *nor* the sister city resolution received its second reading today.
  a. preposition
  b. adverb
  c. pronoun
  d. conjunction

_____ 30. The captain ordered John and me to *peel* 2,000 parsnips.
  a. verb
  b. noun
  c. adverb
  d. preposition

_____ 31. *Unless* the company is granted a utility rate reduction, it plans to close its Midville plant.
  a. adverb
  b. preposition
  c. conjunction
  d. pronoun

_____ 32. *Who* is responsible for the ungrammatical graffiti?
  a. adjective
  b. pronoun
  c. noun
  d. adverb

_____ 33. *This* is the way to San Jose.
  a. pronoun
  b. adjective
  c. adverb
  d. noun

_____ 34. *This* plan never will work.
  a. pronoun
  b. adjective
  c. adverb
  d. noun

_____ 35. I absolutely do *not* want to go to Aruba in August.
  a. verb
  b. adverb
  c. interjection
  d. preposition

_____ 36. I hope *that* I never see another parsnip.
  a. adjective
  b. conjunction
  c. pronoun
  d. adverb

_____ 37. What I don't *need* now is frozen tofu.
  a. adjective
  b. adverb
  c. noun
  d. verb

_____ 38. Please seat Tina Turner *next to* me.
  a. preposition
  b. adverb
  c. conjunction
  d. verb

_____ 39. *Whom* do you wish to see?
  a. preposition
  b. noun
  c. pronoun
  d. conjunction

_____ 40. This is *where* I get off.
  a. conjunction
  b. adjective
  c. preposition
  d. adverb

EXERCISE 4

Parts of Speech 3

Purpose: To continue to build recognition of parts of speech.

Reference: *WWC* (4/e), Chapter 2

Instructions: Identify the underlined words in the following passages and write your answers in the spaces provided.

The Hupmobile Z-38: <u>It's</u> not <u>for</u> you <u>unless</u> you can appreciate <u>fine</u> art. It <u>may</u> be the
                (1)   (2)   (3)   (4)   (5)

<u>best-equipped</u>, and it may be <u>less</u> expensive <u>than</u> comparably <u>sized</u> coupes, <u>but</u> <u>its</u>
   (6)   (7)   (8)   (9)   (10) (11)

world-class design will be <u>what</u> <u>wins</u> you over—and over. So, get <u>off</u> <u>that</u> couch and
                          (12)   (13)   (14) (15)

sit in a real masterpiece—the limited <u>edition</u> Hupmobile Z-38.
                                   (16)

1. _____	7. _____	12. _____
2. _____	8. _____	13. _____
3. _____	9. _____	14. _____
4. _____	10. _____	15. _____
5. _____	11. _____	16. _____
6. _____		

<u>Supporting</u> apartheid in any form is <u>akin</u> to <u>sentencing</u> part of the human <u>race</u> to <u>third-class</u>
  (17)   (18)   (19)   (20)   (21)

status, to economic <u>deprivation</u>—and <u>even</u> to death. To <u>support</u> apartheid is to <u>condone</u>
                 (22)   (23)   (24)   (25)

slavery. To tolerate <u>it</u> on economic grounds is <u>sheer</u> blindness. Not to fight apartheid is
                (26)   (27)

<u>tantamount</u> to pleading <u>guilty</u> to moral decay.
  (28)   (29)

17. _____   22. _____   26. _____

18. _____   23. _____   27. _____

19. _____   24. _____   28. _____

20. _____   25. _____   29. _____

21. _____

<u>While</u> New York's <u>Cardinal</u> O'Connor was a mile away, <u>decrying</u> the violence in Ireland,
  (30)   (31)   (32)

gunmen <u>disguised</u> <u>as</u> police killed a 33-year-old <u>member</u> of the Irish Republican Army
        (33)   (34)   (35)

in Belfast. The <u>shooting</u> <u>occurred</u> 48 <u>hours</u> <u>after</u> an IRA bomb killed a Protestant couple
            (36)   (37)   (38) (39)

and <u>their</u> young son.
  (40)

30. _____   34. _____   38. _____

31. _____   35. _____   39. _____

32. _____   36. _____   40. _____

33. _____   37. _____

EXERCISE 5

Parts of Speech 4

Purpose: To further test your recognition of parts of speech and your ability to demonstrate how they are used in sentence construction.

Reference: *WWC* (4/e), Chapter 2

Instructions: Determine the meaning of the following sentences by supplying the missing words according to their functions as parts of speech. Remember that there are several correct (and logical) word choices.

The Holt Bridge draw span _____ _____ _____
(1. verb)   (2. adverb)   (3. prep.)

noon today, _____ a severe traffic jam _____ lasted six hours.
(4. adj.-part.)   (5. rel. pron.)

_____ a _____ campaign requires money _____ guts.
(6. noun-ger.)   (7. adj.)   (8. conj.)

The commissioners announced _____ would _____ contract
(9. pron.)   (10. verb)

awards _____ by their former purchasing agent.
(11. adj.-past part.)

"_____ just a matter of time," the _____ detective told reporters
(12. pron.-verb contraction)   (13. comp. mod., adv.-adj.)

_____ were _____ listening.
(14. rel. pron.)   (15. adv.)

"I don't think that _____ executives should feel _____
(16. pron.)   (17. adj.)

_____ we make such high-level decisions; _____, we should
(18. subord. conj.)   (19. conjunctive adv.)

_____ remember that _____ can change that any time."
(20. adv.)   (21. noun)

_____ voters _____ rejected the _____ expensive
(22. conj.)   (23. adv.)   (24. adv.)

_____ the tax measures, _____ _____ approved a
    (25. prep.)   (26. pron.)   (27. conjunctive adv.)

$12.5 million levy for a vote-by-mail program.

_____ you and _____ , it looks _____ the bond
    (28. prep.)   (29. pron.)   (30. subord. conj.)

_____ security is going to dissolve.
(31. possessive noun)

"We should examine _____ issue _____ deeply," the
               (32. adj.)   (33. adv.)

_____ committee member told _____ colleagues.
(34. compound mod.)   (35. pron.)

EXERCISE 6

Identification of Sentence Elements

Purpose: To master sentence construction by learning to identify various sentence elements, such as subject, verb, object, predicate nominative/adjective and appositive. This will build a foundation for understanding such principles as agreement and case.

Reference: *WWC* (4/e), pp. 33-35.

Instructions: Examine the italicized portion of each sentence and select its correct function from the choices offered.

_____ 1. The purchasing *agent* accepted the bribe.
     a. subject
     b. verb
     c. indirect object
     d. predicate nominative

_____ 2. *Whom* are you looking for?
     a. subject
     b. direct object
     c. object of preposition
     d. predicate nominative

_____ 3. Give *me* the Maltese falcon, please.
     a. subject
     b. object of preposition
     c. direct object
     d. indirect object

_____ 4. She is the party's *preference* for state treasurer.
     a. verb
     b. direct object
     c. predicate nominative
     d. predicate adjective

_____ 5. This contract offer is an insult to *us* workers.
    a. subject
    b. indirect object
    c. object of preposition
    d. appositive of object

_____ 6. By *1945*, World War II was rapidly coming to a close.
    a. subject
    b. indirect object
    c. object of preposition
    d. predicate nominative

_____ 7. This protein supplement tastes *terrible*.
    a. indirect object
    b. predicate adjective
    c. appositive
    d. predicate nominative

_____ 8. This wood is ideal for *building* cabinets.
    a. verb
    b. predicate adjective
    c. indirect object
    d. object of preposition

_____ 9. *Building* cabinets gives one a great sense of accomplishment.
    a. subject
    b. verb
    c. predicate adjective
    d. appositive

_____ 10. Fourteen people *have been indicted* for grand theft.
    a. subject
    b. verb
    c. object of preposition
    d. predicate nominative

_____ 11. *Scanning* the crowd carefully, he moved toward the lectern.
    a. verb
    b. appositive
    c. subject
    d. none of the above is correct

_____ 12. Rebecca Jenkins, the party's *nominee*, will speak tonight at 8.
   a. subject
   b. appositive of subject
   c. predicate nominative
   d. indirect object

_____ 13. His *was* the most ludicrous speech I've heard in years.
   a. transitive verb
   b. linking verb
   c. intransitive verb

_____ 14. Squid and strawberry jam *tastes* terrible.
   a. transitive verb
   b. linking verb
   c. intransitive verb

_____ 15. The gunmen *ordered* the customers to lie down.
   a. transitive verb
   b. linking verb
   c. intransitive verb

_____ 16. The patient *has been* in a coma since last Tuesday.
   a. transitive verb
   b. linking verb
   c. intransitive verb

_____ 17. Would you please *sit* down?
   a. transitive verb
   b. linking verb
   c. intransitive verb

_____ 18. *Whom* did you select as first-place winner?
   a. subject
   b. object of preposition
   c. direct object
   d. appositive of object

_____ 19. Does this ice cream smell *fishy*?
   a. indirect object
   b. predicate adjective
   c. predicate nominative
   d. direct object

_____ 20. He is eager to discuss the *expedition*.
  a. indirect object
  b. object of infinitive phrase
  c. predicate nominative
  d. appositive

_____ 21. I've told *you* never to bother me when I'm bowling.
  a. indirect object
  b. appositive
  c. predicate nominative
  d. direct object

_____ 22. Between you and *me*, we don't stand a chance.
  a. indirect object
  b. object of infinitive phrase
  c. object of preposition
  d. direct object

_____ 23. His biggest ambition is *to learn the "internet."*
  a. object of infinitive phrase
  b. verb phrase
  c. indirect object
  d. predicate nominative

_____ 24. The patient has been in a coma *since* Tuesday.
  a. adverb
  b. preposition
  c. conjunction

_____ 25. Squid and oatmeal as a menu item *requires* a lot of courage.
  a. transitive verb
  b. linking verb
  c. intransitive verb

_____ 26. *His* was the most ludicrous speech I've heard in years.
  a. subject
  b. appositive
  c. predicate nominative

_____ 27. She is the party's preference for state *treasurer*.
  a. predicate nominative
  b. direct object
  c. appositive
  d. objective of preposition

_____ 28. This wood *is* ideal for building cabinets.
   a. verb
   b. object of infinitive phrase
   c. object of preposition

_____ 29. *Rebecca Jenkins*, the party's nominee for treasurer, will speak tonight at 8.
   a. subject
   b. appositive
   c. predicate nominative

_____ 30. I will *rise* early tomorrow.
   a. direct object
   b. linking verb
   c. intransitive verb

_____ 31. *Infected* with hepatitis, the restaurant cook may have spread the virus to as many as 400 patrons.
   a. intransitive verb
   b. subject
   c. none of the above

_____ 32. By 1945, the war was rapidly *coming* to a close.
   a. predicate nominative
   b. verb
   c. none of the above

_____ 33. There are several *people* waiting for you, and they don't look happy.
   a. subject
   b. predicate nominative
   c. direct object

_____ 34. Lately he just prefers to *stay home*.
   a. verb
   b. part of direct object
   c. object of gerund phrase

_____ 35. Hoisting those *bricks* has injured Hal's back.
   a. object of gerund phrase
   b. subject
   c. both *a* and *b* are correct

EXERCISE 7

Identification of Phrases and Clauses

Purpose: To recognize phrases and clauses, to distinguish one from the other and to understand their functions in sentence construction.

Reference: *WWC* (4/e), pp. 35-36.

Instructions: Identify the underlined sections of the following sentences from the choices offered.

_____ 1. <u>Making ice sculptures</u> in the Mojave Desert is her latest challenge.
    a. phrase
    b. clause

_____ 2. He tore his trousers <u>while climbing over the fence</u>.
    a. phrase
    b. clause

_____ 3. Walk and please, <u>look both ways</u> before crossing.
    a. phrase
    b. clause

_____ 4. You'll wonder <u>where the yellow went</u> when you brush your teeth with Pepsodent!
    a. phrase
    b. clause

_____ 5. <u>Just do it!</u>
    a. phrase
    b. clause
    c. sentence fragment

_____ 6. In order to vote in this state, <u>you must register</u> within 30 days of the next ballot date.
    a. dependent (subordinate) clause
    b. independent clause

_____ 7. The next re-creation of the Lincoln-Douglas Debate, <u>which is set for next Tuesday</u>, will be held in Galesburg.
    a. dependent clause
    b. independent clause

_____ 8. <u>One of the nation's richest counties</u> has declared bankruptcy.
   a. dependent clause
   b. independent clause
   c. phrase

_____ 9. He hoisted the banner high while he marched <u>in the annual Knights of Pythagoreus Parade</u>.
   a. participial phrase
   b. prepositional phrase
   c. dependent clause

_____ 10. She quickly discovered that <u>eating a burrito</u> before riding on the "Cyclone" was a bad idea.
   a. phrase (as subject of clause)
   b. phrase (as object of clause)
   c. prepositional phrase

_____ 11. Linus Pauling won a Nobel Prize <u>for his pioneering work with proteins</u>.
   a. dependent clause
   b. independent clause
   c. phrase

_____ 12. <u>After the grueling triathlon in Hawaii</u>, he vowed never to compete again.
   a. dependent clause
   b. independent clause
   c. phrase

_____ 13. The planning commission vetoed the annexation, but <u>the city council agreed to hold a public hearing on the issue</u>.
   a. dependent clause
   b. independent clause
   c. phrase

_____ 14. She admitted having destroyed the evidence <u>before the police arrested her</u>.
   a. dependent clause
   b. independent clause
   c. phrase

_____ 15. The lecturer <u>who is coming to campus next week</u> was a double agent for the FBI.
   a. dependent clause
   b. independent clause
   c. phrase

_____ 16. <u>To be eligible to vote in this state</u> you must register by Oct. 15.

     a. prepositional phrase

     b. gerund phrase

     c. participial phrase

     d. infinitive phrase

_____ 17. <u>Baking in the sun</u> may feel good, but dermatologists say it prematurely ages the skin.

     a. prepositional phrase

     b. gerund phrase

     c. participial phrase

     d. infinitive phrase

_____ 18. <u>Conquering his fear of heights</u>, he scaled the south slope of Mt. Trashmore.

     a. prepositional phrase

     b. gerund phrase

     c. participial phrase

     d. infinitive phrase

_____ 19. The mayor is meeting today <u>with representatives from the city's three high-crime neighborhoods</u>.

     a. prepositional phrase

     b. gerund phrase

     c. participial phrase

     d. infinitive phrase

_____ 20. The clothes <u>lying on the floor</u> are clean.

     a. prepositional phrase

     b. gerund phrase

     c. participial phrase

     d. infinitive phrase

_____ 21. <u>Disgusted with small-town life</u>, she moved to Cleveland.

     a. prepositional phrase

     b. gerund phrase

     c. participial phrase

     d. infinitive phrase

_____ 22. He found that eating a big meal <u>before the test flight</u> had been a bad idea.

     a. prepositional phrase

     b. gerund phrase

     c. participial phrase

     d. infinitive phrase

_____ 23. She planned <u>to write the novel in the evening</u> after covering the police beat all day.
   a. prepositional phrase
   b. gerund phrase
   c. participial phrase
   d. infinitive phrase

_____ 24. In a surprise move this morning, Judge Eva Lundeen opened her courtroom <u>to photographers and television camera crews</u>.
   a. prepositional phrase
   b. gerund phrase
   c. participial phrase
   d. infinitive phrase

_____ 25. Knowing where to find information is often more important than <u>knowing the information itself</u>.
   a. prepositional phrase
   b. gerund phrase
   c. participial phrase
   d. infinitive phrase

_____ 26. <u>Before the film started</u>, she introduced the director to the audience.
   a. noun clause
   b. adjective clause
   c. adverb clause

_____ 27. The book <u>that he ordered last week</u> is a history of community journalism.
   a. noun clause
   b. adjective clause
   c. adverb clause

_____ 28. <u>That her story was corroborated by the priest</u> certainly helped her case.
   a. noun clause
   b. adjective clause
   c. adverb clause

_____ 29. He apparently shot the dog <u>while the radio was blaring</u>.
   a. noun clause
   b. adjective clause
   c. adverb clause

_____ 30. In the dim light she was unable to identify <u>who the burglar was</u>.
   a. noun clause
   b. adjective clause
   c. adverb clause

_____ 31. Denver, <u>the mile-high city</u>, has a serious pollution problem.

    a. gerund phrase

    b. participial phrase

    c. appositive phrase

    d. infinitive phrase

_____ 32. The television reporters, <u>lugging their own camera equipment</u>, squeezed into the tiny council chambers.

    a. gerund phrase

    b. participial phrase

    c. appositive phrase

    d. infinitive phrase

_____ 33. She knew that <u>to win the campaign</u> she had to capture the student vote.

    a. gerund phrase

    b. participial phrase

    c. appositive phrase

    d. infinitive phrase

_____ 34. Joe McGinnis, <u>author of "Fatal Vision,"</u> spent three years researching his subject.

    a. gerund phrase

    b. participial phrase

    c. appositive phrase

    d. infinitive phrase

_____ 35. <u>Fishing for walleyed pike</u> is both his passion and his livelihood.

    a. gerund phrase

    b. participial phrase

    c. appositive phrase

    d. infinitive phrase

EXERCISE 8

Creation of Phrases and Clauses

Purpose: To learn how to construct specific grammatical forms by building on the skill of recognizing phrases and clauses.

Reference: *WWC* (4/e), pp. 35-36

PARTICIPIAL PHRASES

Instructions: For items 1-5, combine the pairs of sentences into single sentences, using the information in one sentence to create a *participial phrase.* Take particular care with punctuation. Please underline the participial phrase.

1. Jackson Industries was determined to shave corporate costs. The corporation sold its cosmetics division.

   _____

   _____

2. The books are lying on the table. They must be returned to the library today.

   _____

   _____

3. The reporter left the courthouse at noon. She decided to check in at the police station.

   _____

   _____

4. Maya Angelou is an American poet and essayist. She was awarded an honorary doctorate last week.

   _____

   _____

5. They hoisted the 20-foot banner. They marched in the animal rights demonstration.

   _____

   _____

APPOSITIVE PHRASES

Instructions: For items 6-10, combine the pairs of sentences into single sentences, transforming the information in one sentence into an appositive phrase. Watch punctuation. Please underline the appositive phrase.

6. Willamette University is located in Salem, Oregon. Salem is the capital of Oregon.

_____

_____

7. Howard Kohn broke the Karen Silkwood story. Kohn is a contributing writer at "Rolling Stone" magazine.

_____

_____

8. Jane Jones is a Bay City attorney. Jones is a candidate for state senate.

_____

_____

9. KLCC-FM is a National Public Radio affiliate. "All Things Considered" is broadcast on that station every night.

_____

_____

10. Leslie Anderson is a sports reporter for the Daily Bugle. Anderson used to be mayor of Bay City.

_____

_____

INDEPENDENT CLAUSES

Instructions: For Items 11-15, underline the *complete* independent clause in each sentence.

Example:

The players who crossed the picket line faced jeers and taunts.

In this example, note that a dependent clause separates the subject of the main clause from its verb and direct objects.

11. People who live in glass houses shouldn't throw stones.
12. I am writing to Fannie Farmer because Betty Crocker never answers my letters.
13. When the fog lifted, the freighter quickly left port, and the submarine trailed quietly behind.
14. Stop in the name of love, before you break my heart.
15. You know very well that I'm never comfortable in Mr. Rogers' neighborhood.

DEPENDENT CLAUSES

Instructions: For Items 16-20, combine each pair of sentences into a single sentence, using the information in one sentence to create a *dependent clause*. Such a combination shows you that the independent clause you choose will be the main part of the sentence, and the dependent clause will be subordinate to it. After you write a sentence, underline the dependent clause.

Example:

This was a wonderful party. However, I would have preferred a simple, quiet dinner instead.

Solution:

<u>Although this was a wonderful party</u>, I would have preferred a simple, quiet dinner instead.
       (dep. clause)

In this example, "I would have preferred a simple, quiet dinner instead" can stand independently. Remember to use a clause, not a phrase, as your subordinate element here.

16. The senator was re-elected by a landslide yesterday. He was the one who was indicted last week for grand theft.

17. She lost the Kow-Tow Dog Chow account. It was because her agency didn't provide the proper research support.

18. Tom's research findings are original and thought-provoking. However, not many of his colleagues seem to agree with his findings.

19. Elizabeth took the inbounds pass from Zane. After doing that, she turned and calmly hit the three-pointer for the win.

20. The rescue workers removed 14 tons of rock from the shaft. Then they drilled a secondary tunnel through four feet of rock, and then they found the trapped miners.

EXERCISE 9

Giving Power and Focus to Verbs

Purpose: To improve verbs that are weak and imprecise; to see the verb as a major building block in sentence clarity.

Reference: *WWC* (4/e), pp. 13-14.

Instructions: Sentences 1-15 suffer from "verb weakness." Strengthen the following sentences by making the verb more straightforward and truly descriptive.

Example:

There will be a march by striking teachers tomorrow, and they will take their demonstration to city hall. The true action is march—why not focus on that and make the sentence simple, direct—and more clear? (Note: You don't have to include all information in the reconstructed sentence—just the most important items.)

The striking teachers will march to city hall tomorrow.

1. A protest against reduction in welfare payments that was proposed by the state was made today by a coalition of welfare recipients called "Citizens for Justice."

   _____

   _____

2. The auditor inspected the tax returns very, very carefully.

   _____

3. The professor said that she would give ample consideration to complaints about the essay exam.

   _____

4. The Smiths were very sorry about the destruction of their neighbor's lawnmower.

   _____

5. She maintained a very tight hold on the life raft.

   _____

6. He ate the quiche quite quickly, almost in a single gulp.

    _____

7. When I have arrived at the age of 85, I have the fervent hope that I will still be healthy and wise.

    _____

    _____

8. The flood waters ran over the banks in a violent surge.

    _____

9. Bill's sports car slid over the icy road in a dangerous skid.

    _____

10. The governor said she would look very carefully at the report and then would personally manage an investigation of the agency.

    _____

    _____

11. Newton wants to take advantage of the intense public interest in these documents and then to make some financial gain.

    _____

    _____

12. Sarah held back her thoughts about the staff reorganization, even though she was bursting to express her anger.

    _____

    _____

13. The "junk bonds" really hurt the pension fund in a devastating way.

    _____

14. Why is it that I always give in to the urge to speak very, very quietly in the library?

    _____

15. Tom and I had a good-natured bargaining dispute over the price of the antique clock.

    _____

Instructions: For items 16-25, replace each of the following phrases with one strong, precise *verb*. Be careful not to change the meaning of the phrase.

Example:

change **imitate the actions of** to **mimic**

16. move forward slowly

_____

17. damage completely

_____

18. support strongly

_____

19. push very forcefully

_____

20. instills deep fear

_____

21. complain constantly

_____

22. read lightly

_____

23. look at angrily

_____

24. lessen the effect

_____

25. praise highly

_____

EXERCISE 10

Strengthening Modifiers

Purpose: To recognize and correct weak, imprecise modifiers; to learn how such precision can help improve sentence clarity.

Reference: *WWC* (4/e), pp. 23-26.

Instructions: Please replace each phrase with a *single* adjective or adverb that is more descriptive and precise than that phrase.

Example:

Very lukewarm is not as descriptive and precise as *tepid.* Simply tacking on an "intensifying" adverb like very doesn't really help the adjective lukewarm.

1. really strong

   _____

2. a lot of

   _____

3. very firm and unyielding

   _____

4. quite cheap and stingy

   _____

5. ridiculous and quite unbelievable

   _____

6. very fast

   _____

7. rather odd and unconventional

   _____

8. very, very small

   _____

9. as carefully as possible

   _____

10. quite far away

   _____

11. very secretly and covertly

_____

12. quite small

_____

13. highly shocking

_____

14. acting with some reservation

_____

15. almost unbelievably pompous

_____

16. really sad

_____

17. squeezed together

_____

18. severely defeated

_____

19. came close to

_____

20. highly pleasurable

_____

21. worried and quite anxious

_____

22. very thick

_____

23. quite shiny and brilliant

_____

24. very firm and determined

_____

25. really tired

_____

EXERCISE 11

Sentence Construction 1

Purpose: To identify and understand various types of sentences.

Reference: *WWC* (4/e), pp. 36-39

Instructions: Identify the sentence type according to this code: a = simple; b = compound; c = complex; d = compound-complex; e = runon; f = fragment.

_____ 1. Do you have any doubt about the selection of the next Cranberry Days prince and princess?

_____ 2. Police followed the suspects for three hours, but they lost them in rush-hour traffic.

_____ 3. You know very well that I'm never comfortable in Mr. Rogers' neighborhood.

_____ 4. Running down the highway with all her might in a downpour that reminded her of that dreadful night in Rangoon.

_____ 5. That omelette tasted like cottage cheese fried in crankcase oil.

_____ 6. We just got this memo from the shipping department; it said that employees heard through the grapevine there no longer would be free twine.

_____ 7. Adjusting her helmet and visor, she began to wonder whether jumping over 10 riding lawnmowers in a school bus was such a great idea.

_____ 8. Surveying the audience and reviewing her notes, she began her speech and quickly lost all traces of nervousness.

_____ 9. The Thompson Foundation, which honors achievement in medical research, has awarded a $1.8 million grant to Civic Hospital.

_____ 10. The judge said she disagreed.

_____ 11. This was a wonderful party, I would have preferred a simple dinner instead.

_____ 12. Please don't move; I'll get help.

_____ 13. Don't move!

_____ 14. Whenever he gets in the mood to exercise, he sits down until the feeling passes.

_____ 15. I thought this plan would work, I'm sorry to say I was wrong.

_____ 16. Thomas, a well-known critic of the judiciary, has announced her candidacy for the legislature.

_____ 17. Who said, "It ain't over till it's over"?

_____ 18. Traffic deaths have fallen by 10 percent, surprising some critics of the National Highway Safety Administration.

_____ 19. Who did you say was calling?

_____ 20. The management position seems to be weakening, and the union's resolve seems to be growing.

_____ 21. The contractor signed the new agreement and began construction.

_____ 22. After the demonstration, 15 students were charged with criminal acts, including resisting arrest, halting emergency vehicles and blocking entrance to public buildings.

_____ 23. This is hardly the time for complaining; it's the perfect time for action!

_____ 24. You'll wonder where the yellow went when you brush your teeth with Pepsodent.

_____ 25. Have you figured out yet whether you're having fun?

EXERCISE 12

Sentence Construction 2

Purpose: To master sentence construction with the four basic sentence types; to practice coordination and subordination of ideas.

Reference: *WWC* (4/e), pp. 36-39

Instructions: Using most or all of the information in each item below, please construct the sentence type as specified.

Example:

Write a <u>simple sentence</u> with this information:

Five people were killed in an accident.

It happened this morning on Interstate 80.

A four-car pileup was involved.

Solution:

Five people died this morning in a four-car accident on Interstate 80.
(One subject [*five people*], one verb [*died*])

1. Write a <u>simple sentence</u> with this information:

    *Orange County is in financial trouble.

    *It may be facing bankruptcy proceedings.

    *The county's problem is linked to poor investment decisions.

    _____

2. Write a <u>compound sentence</u> with this information:

    *The nation's unemployment rate has dropped.

    *That rate dropped by one percent.

    *However, the Consumer Price Index has increased by 3 percent.

    *Both of these figures are based on statistics prepared last month.

    _____

3. Write a <u>complex sentence</u> with this information:

   *The House defeated the president's tax measure today.

   *The Senate also defeated the same measure today.

   *Prior to this vote, the president had been heavily lobbying his congressional allies to support the measure.

   _____

4. Write a <u>compound-complex</u> sentence with this information:

   *Floods have hit the Midwest, especially Illinois and Missouri.

   *This weather has lasted for two weeks and has resulted in 20 deaths.

   *Hundreds of thousands of acres of corn and soybeans are ruined.

   _____

5. Write a <u>simple sentence</u> with this information:

   *Fourteen people have been indicted by a federal grand jury.

   *The indictment stems from investigation of a cocaine ring.

   *The ring was, according to police, a $20 million operation.

   *The operation was centered in Alabama.

   _____

6. Write a <u>compound sentence</u> with this information:

   *Striking Washington Metro train operators have agreed to return to work tomorrow.

   *However, the Metro's machinist union still hasn't settled on a new contract.

   *More than 400 operators had been on strike; more than 150 machinists remain on strike.

   _____

7. Write a <u>complex sentence</u> with this information:

   *A Middleton jury today returned a guilty verdict against Thomas Arthur.

   *On hearing the verdict, Arthur realized he probably would be spending the next 10 years in prison on a manslaughter charge.

   *After hearing the verdict, Arthur started screaming and attacked the Middleton prosecutor.

   _____

8. Write a <u>compound-complex</u> sentence with this information:

   *The stock market rose sharply today.

   *The Dow Jones Industrial Average climbed 20 points to hit 3,815.

   *By the end of the trading day, however, investors were showing concern about another increase in interest rates by the Federal Reserve.

   _____

EXERCISE 13

Sentence Construction 3

Purpose: To focus and combine ideas in sentences; to create order, prominence and subordination in sentences; to understand rhythm created by sentences of varying length.

Reference: *WWC* (4/e), Chapter 3

PHRASES

Instructions: Write *two* sentences based on each group of facts. In your sentences, create the proper order and prominence of information. Sentence 1 should be *complex*; sentence 2 should be *simple*.

Example:

Do you want to know about good value and cars? The Tucker Turismo is a great value (of course). It gives you the best value for your money—and that's worth knowing!

Solution: Sentence 1 (complex):

Do you want to know which car gives you best value for your money?

Solution: Sentence 2 (simple):

It's the Tucker Turismo, of course.

Note: You don't need to use all information in your sentences. Just be sure that sentence 1 has one independent and one dependent clause and that sentence 2 has just one independent clause.

1. An overloaded passenger ferry capsized in a small lake. That happened in Finland today. A government spokesperson said that more than 200 people drowned in the accident and that there were no survivors.

   Sentence 1 (complex):

   _____

   Sentence 2 (simple):

   _____

2. I remember an amusing but somewhat frightening incident. It was when G. Gordon Liddy shared a Los Angeles auditorium stage with Timothy Leary. It was billed as a "cosmic debate."

Sentence 1:

_____

Sentence 2:

_____

3. Elvis Presley was special. He was, many would say, a musical titan. He had a troubled life, however. It was a life marked by drug use.

Sentence 1:

_____

Sentence 2:

_____

4. Nehru and Gandhi were two names to upset the quietude of the British in embattled India. Clearly, India was nearing a state of revolution, at a time when the British colonists spent a great deal of time attending garden parties.

Sentence 1:

_____

Sentence 2:

_____

5. A Bronx social club was packed with people Sunday afternoon. At that time, a fire destroyed the club. Screaming people trying to find relatives hampered efforts by firefighters to rescue people and to fight the fire. In the fire, seven people were killed.

Sentence 1:

_____

Sentence 2:

_____

EXERCISE 14

Subject-Verb Agreement

Purpose: To create sentence harmony and consistency by learning to choose verbs that agree in number with their subjects.

Reference: *WWC* (4/e), pp. 49-58

Instructions: Mark *a* or *b* to reflect the correct verb choice in each of the following sentences.

_____ 1. There *(a) has (b) have* been a steady increase in hate crimes in the city.

_____ 2. The news media *(a) is (b) are* under attack again.

_____ 3. Three million board feet of lumber *(a) was (b) were* exported last year.

_____ 4. Stealing 30 pounds of imported cheeses *(a) was (b) were* their biggest mistake.

_____ 5. Smith is the only one of the witnesses who *(a) has (b) have* come forward to discuss the crime.

_____ 6. None of the accident victims *(a) is (b) are* expected to live through the night.

_____ 7. Half of the emergency supplies *(a) is (b) are* missing.

_____ 8. A number of senators *(a) has (b) have* threatened to boycott the hearing.

_____ 9. Neither the camera nor its lenses *(a) was (b) were* stolen in the robbery.

_____ 10. The United Mine Workers *(a) bargains (b) bargain* for job security.

_____ 11. Politics *(a) is (b) are* a dirty business.

_____ 12. Around the bend and past the first flashing buoy *(a) is (b) are* an anchorage and dock.

_____ 13. There *(a) has (b) have* been many promotions.

_____ 14. The number of unemployed teenagers *(a) rise (b) rises* sharply every summer.

_____ 15. Lifting weights *(a) has (b) have* increased the strength of the tennis players.

_____ 16. The bad condition of the streets *(a) is (b) are* a disgrace.

_____ 17. Murder is one of those horrors that *(a) causes (b) cause* trusting people to lock their doors at night.

_____ 18. The records or the stereo *(a) has (b) have* to go.

_____ 19. The rate of teenage suicides *(a) is (b) are* climbing.

_____ 20. Stealing original editions *(a) is (b) are* his hobby.

_____ 21. A blackbird, as well as three starlings, *(a) is (b) are* nesting in the tree.

_____ 22. Neither the counterfeit stocks nor the forged report *(a) has (b) have* been found.

_____ 23. Each of the brothers *(a) has (b) have* a special talent.

_____ 24. The number of local banks that *(a) has (b) have* survived the recession is small.

_____ 25. He is one of the best rebounders who *(a) has (b) have* ever played in the NBA.

EXERCISE 15

Antecedent Agreement

Purpose: To create unity and consistency within sentences by selecting correct antecedents.

Reference: *WWC* (4/e), pp. 58-60

Instructions: Mark the appropriate letter to reflect the correct choice in each of the following sentences.

_____ 1. According to Thompson, the phenomena never will be explained; **(a) it (b) they** may as well be part of a magic spell.

_____ 2. No one, having seen the devastation of the Columbian earthquake, will ever view **(a) his (b) his or her (c) their** life the same way again.

_____ 3. The International Association of Electrical Workers bargained aggressively for **(a) its (b) their** new contract.

_____ 4. Smythe is the only one of the birdwatchers who didn't lose **(a) his or her (b) their** field glasses.

_____ 5. WCUZ-TV claims to really care about **(a) its (b) their** audience.

_____ 6. The jury returned **(a) its (b) their** unanimous verdict: not guilty.

_____ 7. Either of those women could handle that job by **(a) herself (b) themselves**.

_____ 8. The Metro-Goldwyn-Gaffer Corp. announced today that **(a) it (b) they** would soon hire 500 more employees.

_____ 9. The audience rose to **(a) its (b) their** feet in loud approval.

_____ 10. The vice presidential candidate's speech was forceful, but **(a) he (b) it received** only a lukewarm response.

_____ 11. History is one of those subjects that scarcely **(a) interest (b) interests** her.

_____ 12. None of the prisoners had **(a) his or her sentence (b) their sentences** reduced.

_____ 13. If the media had done **(a) its (b) their** job, we would know more about issues and less about personalities.

_____ 14. Everyone is entitled to **(a) his (b) his or her (c) their** opinion.

_____ 15. The reporter's story was full of color and detail, but the editor was not impressed with **(a) her (b) it**.

_____ 16. The six-member committee submitted **(a) its (b) their** findings today.

_____ 17. Neither of the wines lost **(a) its (b) their** clarity.

_____ 18. All the data held up after technical experts evaluated **(a) it (b) them**.

_____ 19. Zane is the only one of the journalists who **(a) write (b) writes** with flair.

_____ 20. The American Federation of Teachers urged **(a) its (b) their** members not to strike.

_____ 21. Ohio U's 1955 alumni will hold **(a) its (b) their** reunion next month.

_____ 22. The soccer team took **(a) its (b) their** defeat in stride.

_____ 23. The United States and Russia argued that the Bering Sea island was **(a) its (b) their** own.

_____ 24. Either Hepzibah or Prunella will have to put up **(a) her (b) their** money to help me make bail.

_____ 25. The logic of his "theories" cannot support **(a) itself (b) themselves**.

EXERCISE 16

Case 1

Purpose: To create consistency and agreement within sentences by using pronouns in the correct case.

Reference: *WWC* (4/e), Chapter 5

Instructions: Select the correct pronoun in each of the following sentences.

_____ 1. **(a) Who (b) Whom** does he want to dance with?

_____ 2. **(a) Who (b) Whom** did she say shredded the documents?

_____ 3. The man **(a) who (b) whom** police suspect of the robbery has been released on bail.

_____ 4. The man **(a) who (b) whom** police believed committed the robbery has been released on bail.

_____ 5. The jury understood **(a) you (b) your** pleading the Fifth Amendment.

_____ 6. Catching Thomas and **(a) I (b) me** in the act of counterfeiting baseball cards of Willie Mays and Ted Williams was devastating to our parents.

_____ 7. The group doesn't know **(a) who (b) whom** to select as its representative.

_____ 8. To **(a) who (b) whom** do you wish to speak ?

_____ 9. The guard detained **(a) us (b) we** reporters at the plant gate.

_____ 10. Don't you agree that **(a) us (b) we** freelance writers should form a guild?

_____ 11. Those who have recently moved should ensure that **(a) their (b) they're** registered to vote.

_____ 12. The governor has announced **(a) who (b) whom** she has appointed to the watchdog committee.

_____ 13. This is mine; which is **(a) yours (b) your's**?

_____ 14. **(a) Who (b) Whom** did he say was responsible?

_____ 15. **(a) Your (b) You're** going to be very sorry if you eat that foot-long pickle.

_____ 16. She is much more creative than **(a) I (b) me**.

_____ 17. Please give this message to **(a) whoever (b) whomever** calls at the office at precisely 1 p.m.

_____ 18. **(a) Who's (b) Whose** going to report on this trial?

_____ 19. She is the only candidate **(a) who (b) whom** the union supports.

_____ 20. Everyone agrees there is no better candidate than **(a) her (b) she**.

_____ 21. The books were distributed among **(a) us (b) we** students.

_____ 22. That was he, not **(a) I (b) me**, at the concert.

_____ 23. **(a) Who (b) Whom** did he call a bigot?

_____ 24. Tell that armadillo to learn **(a) its (b) it's** position on the animal rights debate.

_____ 25. **(a) Hers (b) Her's** is the apartment on the third floor.

_____ 26. **(a) You're (b) Your** spastic coughing infuriated the speaker.

_____ 27. Jamie is a hardworking reporter, just like you and **(a) I (b) me**.

_____ 28. It was **(a) he (b) him** who complained to the neighbors.

_____ 29. **(a) Who's (b) Whose** computer has the most memory?

_____ 30. **(a) Who (b) Whom** did he say won the race?

EXERCISE 17

Case 2

Purpose: To continue to build understanding of the proper use of case and to improve editing abilities.

Reference: *WWC* (4/e), Chapter 5

Instructions: Carefully read each of the following sentences. Correct all errors in case and in pronoun selection. Watch for improper use of subject-verb contractions and possessives. Make your changes on this sheet. If the sentence is correct, put a *C* before the number.

_____ 1. The media generally have a difficult time making up there minds on an issue;

however, after listening to the witness's story, its clear they are all confused about

him pleading guilty.

_____ 2. If I were him, I'd consider another line of work; this commissions pace is too hec-

tic.

_____ 3. Why did you inform they rather than I about the incident?

_____ 4. Harris's poll results got a lot of attention, but the politicians don't seem impressed

by him.

_____ 5. Was it him who pointed out we reporters to the security guards?

_____ 6. It was her whom the company put on it's blacklist.

_____ 7. She is a celebrity whom Truman Capote once described as "a cat with a cold."

_____ 8. Guess whom we saw today?

_____ 9. John and Jane's bicycles have been stolen, but their pretty sure about who to suspect.

_____ 10. She is much brighter than me, but our's is still a special relationship.

_____ 11. Your going to be amused by the performance us boys are going to give.

_____ 12. Police have arrested a man whom they say is responsible for the warehouse fires. They're main lead developed yesterday, but it's details aren't being revealed.

_____ 13. Between you and I, its just a matter of time until the finger of suspicion points at us lobbyists.

_____ 14. The market plunged to it's lowest point in three years as a result of this mornings' announcement about the trade deficit.

_____ 15. Whose going to be the first to present their paper on women's rights? I won't stand for you delaying anymore.

_____ 16. Its right their in the paper: The bank will pay $10,000 to whomever is responsible for recovery of the bonds.

_____ 17. Please don't tell dad who I danced with.

_____ 18. Ask not for whom the bell tolls.

_____ 19. Richard Franklin, who's conviction for arson was overturned last month, was killed last night by an intruder who's identity remains unknown.

_____ 20. Its us reporters who have to answer to our editors.

EXERCISE 18

Parallel Structure

Purpose: To improve grammatical consistency by creating parallelism in series, tense, gender and voice.

Reference: *WWC* (4/e), pp. 61–64

Instructions: Some of the following sentences contain errors in parallel structure. If you think the sentence is correct as written, please put a *C* in the space provided. For the other sentences, please rewrite to ensure correct parallelism.

Example: In the sentence **The council approved the new library bonds, but the jail repair measure was defeated by them** there is a problem of mixed voice: active in the first clause, passive in the second. By putting both clauses in the active voice (which is far more direct), the sentence becomes properly parallel in construction:

The council **approved** the new library bonds but **defeated** the jail repair measure.

(You should note that when parallelism is improved, so often are sentence clarity and economy.)

_____ 1. A professor does not always know what is good for his students.

_____

_____ 2. Sarah received the society's Lifetime Achievement Award for her many financial contributions to AIDS research and because she has frequently donated legal services to AIDS patients who are being refused medical treatment.

_____

_____

_____

_____ 3. A student who enjoys the adventure of research and to appreciate the fun of problem-solving should enroll in this course.

_____

_____

_____ 4. The most important aspects of successful teaching are concern for students, preparation of properly targeted material and being sure to follow up on the classroom feedback that one receives.

_____

_____

_____ 5. If you are driven to perfection and not crestfallen by failure, you could succeed in this job.

_____

_____ 6. Your infuriating habit of transcribing your interview tapes and she insisting on hiring two proofreaders will cause us to miss deadlines and great anxiety as well.

_____

_____

_____ 7. Her speech was strident but has that quality that can really uplift.

_____

_____ 8. Everyone is entitled to his or her own opinion.

_____

_____ 9. As soon as this business of yours is placed on firm footing by you, you will start to enjoy the fruits of entrepreneurship.

_____

_____

_____ 10. Think about it: If you have strong organization and are persistent, you will get the client's account.

_____

_____ 11. One should never bet on an incumbent officeholder these days; we should certainly know better than that.

_____

_____

_____ 12. The candidate pledged to lower taxes, reduce welfare spending and that he would support the construction of more state prisons.

_____

_____

_____ 13. Glenn's account presentation was far more innovative and full of humor than what Tom presented.

_____

_____ 14. The mayor discussed next year's revenue forecast, new procedures for zoning variances and that the apartment vacancy rate is declining.

_____

_____

_____ 15. Climbing over the barbed wire fence, his new Armani coat was torn.

_____

EXERCISE 19

Eliminating Sexism in Writing

Purpose: To ensure equal treatment of sexes in writing by identifying and eliminating sexism in language.

Reference: *WWC* (4/e), Chapter 10

Instructions: All of the following sentences contain sexist references (demeaning treatment, dependence on the generic *he*, courtesy titles for women, stereotypes). Please identify the problem below each sentence and then rewrite it to ensure equal treatment of the sexes.

Example: In sentence 1 of Exercise 18 ("A professor does not always know what is good for his students"), the error is the use of the generic *he*. Not all professors are males, and it is both erroneous and demeaning to presume maleness when the sex of the antecedent is not stated. A simple correction can be made—change *professor* to plural and use a plural possessive:

Professors do not always know what is good for their students.

1. The lady electrician completed the wiring job in less than two hours.

   _____

   _____

2. She's a fine sailboat; however, she's difficult to maneuver occasionally and always a great expense.

   _____

   _____

3. Everyone is entitled to their opinion.

   _____

   _____

4. Mrs. Harold (Hilda) Thomas preceded her husband in death by two years.

   _____

   _____

5. He's a great mechanic—a real expert on Plymouths like yours; he should have her ready this afternoon.

   _____

   _____

6. Police Lt. Thomas Jefferson and Miss Mary Kay Forgeron, a patrolman, addressed the high school convocation.

   _____

   _____

7. An Ohio man and his wife have been selected to appear on the nationally syndicated "Know Your Spouse" television show.

   _____

   _____

8. John Thomas, branch manager of the Second Interstate Bank, and Susan Thiene, a pert, trim divorcée who is owner of the Thiene Publishing Co., have been selected as cochairmen of the United Way drive.

   _____

   _____

9. Thomason was convicted yesterday of the deaths of two Stephens College coeds who were strangled last August.

   _____

   _____

10. The coach can restore the enthusiasm and wonder of the young boy in all of us.

    _____

    _____

11. Walt Whitman was a male nurse during the Civil War.

    _____

    _____

12. The lady mechanic and her boss made a gentleman's agreement about her working hours and pay.

    _____

    _____

13. The Clarksons have been man and wife for 55 years.

    _____

    _____

14. The Moline String Quartet, which contains three females, will appear Jan. 12 at the Hillyer Center.

    _____

    _____

15. Every American should exercise his right to vote.

    _____

    _____

EXERCISE 20

Proper Use of Voice

Purpose: To learn to write more forcefully and crisply by using active voice constructions; to identify the occasional construction that is better served by passive voice.

Reference: *WWC* (4/e), Chapter 6

Instructions: Active voice makes the subject of the sentence perform. In your writing, you should make the subject *act* rather than being *acted on*. In the following passive voice sentences (1) circle the agent who or that performs the action, (2) underline the object or receiver of the action and (3) rewrite the sentence in the active voice, unless passive voice is more effective in that particular example. If you make no change, explain your decision.

Example:

The election was won by Boxer.

Boxer won the election.

1. An investigation of stolen stockpiles of nuclear waste is being made by the Senate subcommittee.

   _____

2. The tapestry was restored by hundreds of artisans.

   _____

3. Mayor Herman Munster was assaulted and robbed by three men in masks.

   _____

4. The Thompson murder trial is underway today, and it is being presided over by Judge J.T. Frei.

   _____

5. There was a belching noise made by Cool Hand Luke.

   _____

6. At dawn, the crowing of a rooster was heard.

   _____

7. Allegations of impropriety were repeatedly denied by the press secretary of Donovan.

_____

8. Delegates were told by the UNESCO director that elimination of funding by the United States would cripple the organization.

_____

9. There is a special defense appropriation measure that will be considered by the House Armed Services Committee.

_____

10. The thick smoke around the house was being dodged by the wary firefighters.

_____

11. Former city councillor Tim Jewell was arrested last night for drunken driving.

_____

12. He was robbed by a knife-wielding teenager.

_____

13. It has been proved repeatedly by government studies that wearing seat belts saves lives.

_____

14. Tons of deadly plutonium particles were carried by brisk winds.

_____

15. At dusk, the cries of a wounded animal were heard.

_____

16. More than $2 million in negotiable bonds were stolen this morning at the Second Interstate Bank by a man on stilts wearing a Pee-Wee Herman mask.

_____

17. The football was thrown 70 yards from the quarterback to the wide receiver.

_____

18. Her decision was to sit at home quietly until she received word of the election results; and that's just what was done by her.

_____

19. There were rotten plums scattered all over the yard.

_____

20. He is called a conservative in a progressive's disguise by his Senate colleagues.

_____

EXERCISE 21

Restrictive and Non-Restrictive Constructions

Purpose:: To learn the difference between restrictive and non-restrictive constructions in order to select correct relative pronouns and punctuation for them.

Reference: *WWC* (4/e), Chapter 5

PART ONE

Instructions: Identify the underlined section in sentences 1-10 according to the following code: a = restrictive clause; b = non-restrictive clause; c = restrictive phrase; d = non-restrictive phrase.

_____ 1. He is the kind of candidate <u>who is easy to forget</u>.

_____ 2. Harmonicas <u>that are made of plastic</u> don't have that tinny sound I've grown to love.

_____ 3. Sharman's Artichokes, <u>which has become the standard of the industry</u>, is a California success story.

_____ 4. His broker, <u>the fast-track firm of Insiders. Inc.,</u> has recently attracted the attention of the SEC.

_____ 5. This is the person <u>who police said is their main suspect</u>.

_____ 6. "Citizen Kane," <u>Orson Welles' greatest cinematic achievement</u>, was not a financial success in its first release.

_____ 7. The dogs <u>that have been attacking area sheep</u> have been killed.

_____ 8. His sister <u>Karen</u> will attend law school this fall.

_____ 9. Presidential campaigns,<u> which receive massive federal support</u>, are not for the faint of heart.

_____ 10. The investigators <u>who were sent by the insurance firm</u> have already filed their reports.

PART TWO

Instructions: Using some of the facts provided here, write the following sentences: one with a non-restrictive clause, one with a restrictive clause and one with a non-restrictive appositive phrase.

Facts: Police shot John Jones, 23, dead today after a brief gun battle at his Lincoln home. Police say that he was a suspect in seven arson-related murders in three Midwestern states. Police arrested Tim Jones, 19, at the scene. Tim is a brother of John. Tim was charged with assault and obstruction. Tim was not injured in the shooting. Police found $200,000 in cash on the premises. They believe the money is part of payoffs in the arson incidents.

11. Sentence with a non-restrictive clause:

_____

_____

12. Sentence with a restrictive clause:

_____

_____

13. Sentence with a non-restrictive appositive phrase:

_____

_____

EXERCISE 22

That/Which/Who and Restrictive/ Non-Restrictive Constructions

Purpose: To identify restrictive and non-restrictive clauses and to make correct decisions about punctuation and relative pronoun choices in the writing of these constructions.

Reference: *WWC* (4/e), Chapter 5

PART ONE

Instructions: Identify the following underlined constructions in items 1-5 according to this legend: R= Restrictive; NR = Non-Restrictive

_____ 1. The stocks <u>that my broker has recommended</u> have gone bust.

_____ 2. Don't forget: You promised to deliver the tofu brownies <u>that are on the grand piano</u> to the protein crisis support group.

_____ 3. Don't forget: <u>You promised</u> to get me to the church on time.

_____ 4. <u>After he delivered the brownies,</u> he headed to Cleveland.

_____ 5. His special-effects animation process, <u>which he patented in 1995,</u> is eagerly sought by all the major studios.

PART TWO

Instructions: For items 6-18, please select the correct pronoun (with appropriate punctuation and subject-verb agreement) from the choices offered.

_____ 6. Digital photography (a)**, which** is yet to be perfected, (b) **that** is yet to be perfected (c) **which** is yet to be perfected shows great promise in all media.

_____ 7. What did you think of that digital photograph (a) **that** (b) **which** was published in last month's issue of "Wired"?

_____ 8. The stock certificates (a) **that** (b) **which** were mailed to the brokerage house today are counterfeit.

_____ 9. The anti-abortion activist (a) **that** (b) **who** was arrested at the Charleston clinic has now been charged with assault.

_____ 10. Sally is the only one of the reporters (a) **who have** (b) **that have** (c) **who has** (d) **that has** refused to respond to the subpoena.

_____ 11. Shallots (a)**, that** belong to the onion family, (b) **which** belong to the onion family (c)**, which** belong to the onion family, (d) **who** belong to the onion family are a tender delicacy.

_____ 12. Personal income tax returns, (a) **that** (b) **which** are always due in April, are not a pleasant harbinger of spring.

_____ 13. This is one of those offers (a) **that** (b) **which** make fools of the greedy.

_____ 14. Auto workers (a) **who** (b) **that** (c) **which** have accumulated 25 years of service are eligible for the special medical supplement policy.

_____ 15. Sores (a)**, which** do not heal normally, (b) **that** do not heal normally can be a warning signal of cancer.

_____ 16. The woman (a) **that** (b) **who** (c) **whom** police said vandalized the Ann Arbor Library has been arrested in Toledo.

_____ 17. Police have not yet identified the suspect (a) **that** (b) **who** (c) **whom** (d)**, whom** they consider armed and dangerous.

_____ 18. Derek continues to be baffled by a problem (a) **which** (b) **that** punishes far more than it intrigues.

PART THREE

Instructions: Using some of the facts provided, please write the following sentences:

one with a clause that uses the relative pronoun *that*

one with a clause that uses the relative pronoun *which*

Facts: Torrential rains have caused a series of mud slides on U.S Highway 101 in Northern California today. One slide has covered 800 yards of the highway and has blocked all traffic for more than eight miles in either direction. That slide has resulted in one death. The body of Thomas Prince, 42, of Susanville, was discovered this afternoon in the debris of mud and trees in a slide just north of Crescent City.

19. Sentence using a clause with the relative pronoun *that*:

_____

_____

20. Sentence using a clause with the relative pronoun *which*:

_____

_____

EXERCISE 23

Punctuation 1

Purpose: To bring clarity and meter to your writing by making correct punctuation choices.

Reference: *WWC* (4/e), Chapter 7

Instructions: Complete the following sentences by selecting the correctly punctuated choice.

_____ 1. The fielder grabbed the ground ball **(a) but (b), but** she was unable to throw it home in time.

_____ 2. She is a **(a) widely-traveled (b) widely traveled** consultant.

_____ 3. The much-feared hurricane has moved on **(a) but (b); but (c), but** heavy rainstorms have followed in its wake.

_____ 4. Smith struggled to **(a) victory, (b) victory;** however, several runners collapsed from the heat.

_____ 5. It's going to be another **(a) long Arctic (b) long, Arctic** night.

_____ 6. He is a **(a) well educated (b) well-educated** person.

_____ 7. Journalists are only human **(a), nevertheless, (b); nevertheless (c); nevertheless,** readers expect perfection.

_____ 8. The district attorney called the **(a) defendant (b) defendant,** "a cold-blooded killer of young innocents."

_____ 9. Have you seen **(a) "Bambi?" (b) "Bambi"?**

_____ 10. He was elected to the House **(a) but (b), but (c); but** he received only minor committee assignments.

_____ 11. If you are going to learn anything about punctuation, it should be **(a) this, commas (b) this: commas (c) this: Commas** are often misused.

_____ 12. We'll have to suspend this project **(a), because (b) because** of the public protest.

_____ 13. The United Nations has approved a new aid package for Somalia **(a) which (b), which** is suffering from a war-induced famine.

_____ 14. The council discussed new sewer rates, annexation procedures **(a) and (b), and** appointment of a labor grievance committee.

_____ 15. It's going to be another **(a) hot humid (b) hot, humid, (c) hot, humid** day.

_____ 16. Have you read this morning's **(a) New York Times? (b) "New York Times?"** **(c) "New York Times"?**

_____ 17. Have you finished **(a) War and Peace (b) "War and Peace"** yet?

_____ 18. "Voters won't stand for such excessive spending **(a) practices", (b) practices,"** Thompson told the commissioners.

_____ 19. The governor returned today from her trade mission **(a) having (b), having** arranged three contracts for heavy machinery exports.

_____ 20. She asked, **(a) Where's the Ben Gay? (b) "Where's the Ben Gay"? (c) "Where's the** **Ben Gay?"**

_____ 21. I won't support your project **(a) because (b) , because** your business plan is incomplete.

_____ 22. She told the judge **(a) , "to stand for justice and not for business". (b) "to stand for** **justice and not for business."**

_____ 23. Do you support **(a) women's (b) womens'** rights?

_____ 24. **(a) One fourth (b) One-fourth** of the county's investment portfolio has been wiped out.

_____ 25. **(a) It's (b) Its (c) Its'** just a matter of time.

EXERCISE 24

Punctuation 2

Purpose: To continue learning to make correct punctuation choices.

Reference: *WWC* (4/e), Chapter 7

PART ONE

Instructions: Choose the one *correctly punctuated sentence* from each group of choices.

_____ 1. a. He was forced to make a last minute decision.

      b. She is a highly-regarded consultant.

      c. I'm going to postpone this decision it's too important to make under time pressure.

      d. The attorney called the case, "a tragedy that was just waiting to happen."

_____ 2. a. If I were he, I'd study harder.

      b. I oppose this resolution, because it flies in the face of the city charter.

      c. I remember "The New Deal;" it was a historic time for our country.

      d. She's a dedicated teacher, and a fine friend.

_____ 3. a. This is one of those cars, that needs a tune-up every 5,000 miles.

      b. You were in class when Professor Moriarty brought in the cadaver, weren't you, Tom?

      c. I'll have to object again, because this motion is entirely out of order.

      d. Janet has taken a reporting job at the "Los Angeles Times."

_____ 4. a. Dead are John Smith, 37, of New York City, and Angela Ruiz, 33, of Denver.

      b. As I recall, the three items on my shopping list are tofu, sardines—and bean sprouts.

      c. I've always considered her a good-natured person.

      d. "Let's remember who caused this problem", Smith said.

_____ 5. a. I can't figure out this dangerous irrational stock market.

      b. The Broncos responded with a 75-yard, 10-play scoring march.

      c. Did you understand that article (especially the part about supply-side economic?).

      d. Now pay attention to this: we all have to take two day's unpaid leave.

_____ 6. a. The armadillo that ate my lunch is now a pair of shoes.

b. He's a wonderful guy, however, he's poor.

c. She watches only public TV shows (the kind sponsored by oil companies.)

d. The man, whom police suspected of the robbery, has been found strangled in Brooklyn.

_____ 7. a. This legislation shows some promise; nevertheless I must vote against it.

b. The Olympic commitee chose Jefferson, Davis, and Lee.

c. The parade was supposed to wind through the business district; but it missed its turn and ended up on the beach.

d. Thompson, who declared her candidacy just three weeks ago, had a surprisingly strong showing; but it wasn't enough to upset the incumbent.

_____ 8. a. Smith, herself, will head the commission.

b. "Why should we pay these taxes?" Smith asked.

c. He tried a desperation shot but the 45-foot toss fell well short of its mark.

d. The 37-year-old candidate asked: "Are you really better off than you were two years ago"?

PART TWO

Instructions: Read the following sentences to see whether they contain errors in punctuation. If you think a sentence has an error, choose an answer that corrects it. If you think the sentence is correct, choose c—Sentence is correct as is.

_____ 9. "Fight all unfair taxes!" the candidate urged the audience in a strongly worded attack.

a. Comma needed after quotation marks.

b. Hyphen needed between *strongly* and *worded*.

c. Sentence is correct as is.

_____ 10. Long thought to be relatively flat and shaped like huge Frisbees, some galaxies actually are oblong in shape, this has prompted some scientists to call for more studies.

a. Comma splice creates a run-on sentence.

b. Comma needed between *flat* and *and*.

c. Sentence is correct as is.

_____ 11. Did you see that article in "Mother Jones" magazine? I did—and believe me, it had a tremendous impact.

a. Replace dash with semicolon.

b. Remove quotation marks from magazine title.

c. Sentences are correct as they are.

_____ 12. Connie Smith says she's ready "to stand on a stump and shout" if that's what it takes to get the commission's attention.

    a. Apostrophe not needed for _commission_.

    b. Quotation marks must be eliminated.

    c. Sentence is correct as is.

_____ 13. She enjoys sailing, but would rather avoid the boating resorts that so many well-heeled tourists enjoy.

    a. No comma needed between _sailing_ and _but_.

    b. Hyphen not needed after _well_.

    c. Sentence is correct as is.

_____ 14. She told the audience, "Fight for your rights! Don't let these fascists control your lives!"

    a. Last exclamation mark should be outside quotation marks.

    b. Replace comma after _audience_ with colon.

    c. Sentence is correct as is.

_____ 15. Labor and management incidentally have not had an easy contract settlement in the 45-year history of this plant.

    a. Hyphen not needed between _45_ and _year_.

    b. _Incidentally_ is a parenthetical remark and must be set off with commas.

    c. Sentence is correct as is.

EXERCISE 25

Punctuation 3

Purpose: To focus on proper use of commas, semicolons and colons through an editing exercise.

Reference: *WWC* (4/e), pp. 88-99

Instructions: Punctuate the following 20 sentences with corrections as needed with the use of commas, semicolons or colons. If a sentence is correct, mark it with a *C*.

Example:

He told the audience, in no uncertain terms, "We simply will not abide your barbaric behavior. Shut up or go home"!

_____ 1. He failed the entrance exam, because he could not complete more than 70 percent of the questions, in the required time.

_____ 2. He failed the exam; but he vowed to pass it the next time.

_____ 3. Although he failed the exam; he vowed to pass it the next time, however his friends worried he would never attempt the test again.

_____ 4. Harney County farmers grow alfalfa barley and hops.

_____ 5. I really don't understand your excuse; however, I'll accept your paper this time.

_____ 6. "However" the professor added emphatically I'm never ever late".

_____ 7. When the clock struck twelve the students could think of only one thing, sleep.

_____ 8. Don't lecture me about civic responsibility; your voting record is more threadbare than my old dog's blanket.

_____ 9. The two elderly women who I am told always use public transportation have published five best-sellers in the last three years.

_____ 10. The swollen raging Sacramento River is threatening several California towns and the U.S. Army Reserve is preparing for emergency evacuations.

_____ 11. While the children were eating the mosquitoes swarmed around the table.

_____ 12. Tobias himself will present the report which will be broadcast on the C-SPAN network.

———— 13. Smith said they would "get rich quick" Jones said they'd "get dead quicker".

———— 14. You'll like him, he's a Leo who enjoys tofu on just about anything.

———— 15. The witness said the district attorney was, "an opportunist who would convict his own mother if it guaranteed his re-election".

———— 16. The defense attorney asked: "How can you convict someone on such thin, circumstantial evidence"?

———— 17. Schmidt the former standout third baseman for the Phillies was an easy, first-vote choice for the Hall of Fame.

———— 18. Present at the meeting were Thomas Haley councillor for the First Ward, Sarah Henderson district attorney for Linn County, Ralph Petersen chair of the city planning commission, and Richard Rayburg president of the Butte Chamber of Commerce.

———— 19. To the governor all the crises of the past three years added up to just one solution, more tax revenue.

———— 20. After he left the meeting, when the demonstration threatened to turn violent the network television crew arrived to document the anarchy.

EXERCISE 26

Punctuation 4

Purpose: To learn how to use all punctuation marks correctly.

Reference: *WWC* (4/e), Chapter 7

Instructions: Punctuate the following sentences as needed. If a sentence is correct, mark it *C*.

_____ 1. She is a good natured employee are you?

_____ 2. The Celtics flew home, having won all six of their road games.

_____ 3. Although she moved to Hartford she stayed in contact with all her widely-scattered friends.

_____ 4. The newly elected senator is well-spoken and widely read.

_____ 5. He moved to Dallas because he needed a challenge, however he was sorely disappointed.

_____ 6. Did you see the movie remake of Little Women?

_____ 7. I didnt do it! How can you accuse me of killing my own kin the defendant screamed!

_____ 8. The following items are on tomorrows agenda electing officers setting a regular meeting time deciding on fund raising activities and amending the charter.

_____ 9. I hate waiting in lines especially for movies however this is one film I just cant miss.

_____ 10. He was bright successful and dead.

_____ 11. To Billy Jack was above reproach.

_____ 12. The book thats on reserve is required reading, the material will be on the midterm exam according to Professor Smith.

_____ 13. Since the tax levy failed, Lincoln High Schools teachers have been boycotting classes.

_____ 14. Forty senators serve us in this states assembly, 26 men and 14 women.

_____ 15. He's tried running the marathon several times but has never finished.

_____ 16. The woman who was standing in line was angry.

_____ 17. He said to "forget the whole thing" however we felt certain that these "things" could not the forgotten.

_____ 18. The review of the movie Pulp Fiction in the Centerville Gazette was well written.

_____ 19. The reporter found four sources and interviewed two of them.

_____ 20. I'm not embarrassed to say this Gumby was well liked in my neighborhood.

_____ 21. The sisters in laws' agreement to meet again in five years fell apart just three months' later.

_____ 22. I dream of the so called ideal job often; short on hours and long on pay.

_____ 23. The more I see of this proposal, the less I like it.

_____ 24. "Get moving!", the police shouted at the demonstrators.

_____ 25. I could do this, if I had the proper training.

Name _____ Score _____

EXERCISE 27

Subordination and Modification

Purpose: To improve clarity and readability of sentences by improving the coordination of ideas through proper subordination and modification.

Reference: *WWC* (4/e), Chapter 9

Instructions: Edit (or rewrite) the following sentences to eliminate oversubordination, split constructions and/or confusing modifications.

Example:

While sprinting around the track, her long braids whipped in the wind.

This is confusing modification—*are her braids really sprinting around the track*? It is more clear to write

With her long braids whipping in the wind, she sprinted around the track.

1. The magazine story libeled Bob Carey, who was a state senator at the time, who then lost his bid for re-election.

   _____

   _____

2. People who eat fish frequently have low blood cholesterol levels.

   _____

3. The store almost sold out every new edition of the "Monster-Meister" video games.

   _____

4. The organic farm collective, which has 45 members, cast their votes with 38 yeas, 4 against and with 3 members abstaining, that resulted in its banning the use of any pesticides.

   _____

   _____

5. The House approved yesterday in a vote whose tie had to be broken by the Speaker a bill to require the registration of all garden tools with the nearest county sheriff.

   _____

   _____

6. When she began her career, which was as a nightclub singer, while she was only a teenager, Patsy Brown had trouble dealing with her stage fright.

_____

_____

7. City officials have promised for more than two years to clean up the toxic waste dump.

_____

8. Those who lie often are found out.

_____

9. Because he needed the money, Nick took the bribe, although he knew he shouldn't.

_____

10. After reading the Sunday comics in the hot tub, the ink ran all over his hands and arms.

_____

11. The planning commission, after listening to public testimony for an hour and then debating the issue for two hours, denied the application to build a homeless shelter near the high school.

_____

_____

12. If because her business calls for it and she has to travel, then she will.

_____

13. He pledged to as soon as he could form the committee to investigate the growing problem of welfare fraud.

_____

_____

14. I realized that I had spent after the county fair had left town my life's savings on the basketball toss.

_____

15. Even after he landed the job, which seemed to fit his education and qualifications and which promised to make use of his special talents, he was still depressed.

_____

_____

EXERCISE 28

Word Use 1

Purpose: To add consistency and logic to writing by preserving the distinctive meaning of words.

Reference: *WWC* (4/e), Chapter 9

Instructions: Make the correct word choice from the alternatives offered in the sentences.

_____ 1. **(a) Compared to (b) Compared with** last year's record, this year's stock performance is terribly weak.

_____ 2. Labor arbitrators should be **(a) disinterested (b) uninterested** parties in collective bargaining disputes.

_____ 3. Twelve **(a) people (b) persons** were killed in weekend accidents.

_____ 4. Potatoes **(a) that (b) which** are grown in Idaho have a national reputation for quality.

_____ 5. **(a) Because (b) Since** you failed to mail the warranty, the company will not honor your request for free repairs.

_____ 6. **(a) Their (b) There** once-invincible stock portfolio is now the weakling of the Dow Jones playground.

_____ 7. What **(a) implication (b) inference** can you draw from his thinly veiled charges?

_____ 8. It's only about six miles **(a) farther (b) further** to camp.

_____ 9. The nuclear freeze demonstration attracted **(a) more than (b) over** 10,000 students.

_____ 10. I don't believe that the plaintiff has **(a) proved (b) proven** his claim.

_____ 11. The faculty senate **(a) censored (b) censured** the dean for her failure to produce a more convincing tenure package for the young professor.

_____ 12. The baseball commissioner is convinced that the game needs **(a) fewer (b) less** free agents.

_____ 13. The candidate compared his opponent **(a) to (b) with** "a toad-sucking snake."

_____ 14. The party **(a) convinced (b) persuaded** her to run for the office.

_____ 15. The motor scooter (a) **crashed** (b) **collided** into the parked car.

_____ 16. In reading the prepared text of your speech, I sense that you are (a) **implying** (b) **inferring** that all military aid should be taken away from countries in violation of the treaty.

_____ 17. How do you explain his (a) **reluctance** (b) **reticence** to sign the contract?

_____ 18. The prisoner was (a) **hanged** (b) **hung** by the lynch mob.

_____ 19. How do you think this price rise will (a) **affect** (b) **effect** our sales projections?

_____ 20. The meeting will (a) **occur** (b) **take place** as scheduled.

_____ 21. (a) **Because of** (b) **Due to** the blizzardlike conditions at the Mount Hood pass, the ski team will delay its regular weekly conditioning trip.

_____ 22. This award-winning recipe is (a) **composed of** (b) **comprised of** seven "secret" ingredients.

_____ 23. She is (a) **anxious** (b) **eager** to present her findings to the committee.

_____ 24. You look (a) **as if** (b) **like** you've been watching too many political advertisements.

_____ 25. The candidate's staff was embarrassed that he (a) **alluded** (b) **eluded** to the controversial spending report.

EXERCISE 29

Word Use 2

Purpose: To continue to recognize the distinctive meaning of words.

Reference: *WWC* (4/e), Chapter 9

Instructions: Make the correct word choice for each sentence.

_____ 1. Your efforts to **(a) convince (b) persuade** me have failed.

_____ 2. I don't believe you have **(a) proved (b) proven** your point.

_____ 3. The press conference will **(a) occur (b) take place** at noon tomorrow.

_____ 4. **(a) Because (b) Since** he crossed the picket line, some strikers attacked him and burned his car.

_____ 5. This course should be offered for **(a) fewer (b) less** credits.

_____ 6. Can you tell me **(a) if (b) whether** the housing committee will meet tonight?

_____ 7. How do you think this tropical storm will **(a) affect (b) effect** your travel plans?

_____ 8. Bumstead compared the drop in stock prices **(a) to (b) with** a 10,000-foot free fall from a hot-air balloon.

_____ 9. **(a) Because of (b) Due to** the sudden drop in stock prices, companies are buying back shares from a wary public.

_____ 10. It looks **(a) as if (b) like** your proposal will fail.

_____ 11. The exuberant winner said she was **(a) anxious (b) eager** to begin her legislative duties.

_____ 12. These potatoes taste especially **(a) good (b) well** with sour cream.

_____ 13. The sun was shining **(a) real (b) really** brightly.

_____ 14. His campaign speech **(a) evoked (b) invoked** hearty applause from the National Guard veterans.

_____ 15. Could you **(a) lend (b) loan** me your solar-powered toothbrush?

_____ 16. The football score **(a) that (b) which** was first reported by the news bureau was incorrect.

_____ 17. She is more talented **(a) than (b) then** any other reporter at this newspaper.

_____ 18. **(a) Its (b) It's** just a matter of time, she said.

_____ 19. The committee is **(a) composed of (b) comprised of** four Pulitzer Prize winners.

_____ 20. Madonna and Elvis **(a) alluded (b) eluded** the eager band of photographers.

_____ 21. Your tie is a nice **(a) complement (b) compliment** to your coat.

_____ 22. The tofu salad tastes **(a) terrible (b) terribly**.

_____ 23. The mob **(a) hanged (b) hung** the suspect and burned down the jail.

_____ 24. How does this year's inflation rate **(a) compare to (b) compare with** last year's?

_____ 25. She is **(a) anxious (b) eager** about the test results.

EXERCISE 30

Word Use 3

Purpose: To sharpen precision in word choice by using the editing process to spot and correct word choice errors.

Reference: *WWC* (4/e), Part II

Instructions: Review the following sentences and correct all errors in word choice. Make corrections on these sheets with simple editing marks.

1. The speaker said she was not adverse to attempts to persuade her to change her position.

2. Set down and I'll recite the litany of all my broken principals.

3. This car's sticker price is under $15,000; compared to the cost of a new stegowagon, it's a real steal.

4. Since you are heading this committee, it is obvious that we will not examine this critical issue any farther.

5. Such complements from adoring fans have proven that underwater synthesized music is the future of rock and roll.

6. Over 300 persons composed the city's largest mass gathering against organic foods.

7. What was Bierce's quote about the American public?

8. Don't you realize that the affect of this news will sorely impact our earnings projections?

9. You can be sure that his speech meant to infer that the country is speeding toward double-digit inflation.

10. The work stoppage has effected fewer than three divisions of the company.

11. He has been persuaded to accept the agreement in principle.

12. She is anxious to present her findings on the charter amendment.

13. After he laid down for a while, he said he felt like he was a new man.

14. The economic summit will feature special negotiations among the World Bank, several Third World countries and three private financiers.

15. The senator's aid has repeatedly eluded to a "mysterious foreign force" on the finance sub-committee.

16. What is said to who with what affect?

17. Everyone is entitled to his opinion.

18. The winter hurricane ravished the South Carolina coastline.

19. The school principle reported that over 700 persons have applied for the position of teacher's aid.

20. Due to a failure of their own crops, Russia is expected to import a record amount of Western wheat this year.

21. The press did nothing to counter national euphoria with a more realistic view of a war which ultimately claimed the lives of hundreds of soldiers.

22. Are you persuaded yet of the correctness of my position?

23. The man spent the day just laying around his apartment.

24. I would compare his personality with the fresh, cool breeze of an early spring day.

25. Are you concerned that this recession will have a greater affect on the economy than last year's downturn?

EXERCISE 31

Spelling 1

Purpose: To hone the vital skill of spelling.

Reference: *WWC* (4/e), Chapter 8; your dictionary

Instructions: In each of the four-word sets below, choose the word that is spelled correctly. "Alternate" spellings are considered incorrect.

_____ 1.	a. deterrent	b. wierd	c. acceptabel	d. cancelled
_____ 2.	a. changable	b. advertising	c. amung	d. ocassion
_____ 3.	a. supercede	b. acommodate	c. copywright	d. compelled
_____ 4.	a. definate	b. couragous	c. tarrif	d. embarrass
_____ 5.	a. suprise	b. admissible	c. indispensible	d. annullment
_____ 6.	a. loneliness	b. alottment	c. apall	d. developement
_____ 7.	a. cemetary	b. priviledge	c. questionnaire	d. profitible
_____ 8.	a. parallel	b. persistant	c. withold	d. inferance
_____ 9.	a. caffiene	b. grammer	c. prefered	d. forcible
_____ 10.	a. licence	b. leisure	c. millionnaire	d. petulence
_____ 11.	a. macaber	b. profitted	c. noticeable	d. fullfill
_____ 12.	a. percieve	b. precede	c. temperment	d. resistent
_____ 13.	a. rivetted	b. tranquility	c. legitimit	d. pardonable
_____ 14.	a. proceed	b. kidnapping	c. practised	d. weild
_____ 15.	a. libelling	b. mathmatics	c. unanimous	d. maintainance
_____ 16.	a. neice	b. likible	c. vacillate	d. tendancy
_____ 17.	a. existance	b. dilemna	c. despicible	d. sovereign
_____ 18.	a. atheletic	b. presumable	c. lothe	d. tresspass
_____ 19.	a. ommit	b. broccoli	c. ossillate	d. manuver
_____ 20.	a. newsstand	b. sieze	c. satilite	d. tryed
_____ 21.	a. seperate	b. travelled	c. tonsillitis	d. recurrant
_____ 22.	a. wellcome	b. vaccuum	c. villian	d. accidentally
_____ 23.	a. abridgement	b. adolescent	c. rythm	d. alledged
_____ 24.	a. benifit	b. cieling	c. descendant	d. distributer
_____ 25.	a. chief	b. begger	c. donkies	d. dispair

EXERCISE 32

Spelling 2

Purpose: To continue to improve spelling skills.

Reference: *WWC* (4/e), Chapter 8; your dictionary

Instructions: In each four-word set below, choose the *misspelled* word.

_____	1. a. corroborate	b. sattelite	c. willful	d. parallel
_____	2. a. occurrence	b. committment	c. metallic	d. canceled
_____	3. a. innuendo	b. inoculate	c. gorgeous	d. blugeon
_____	4. a. allottment	b. occasional	c. recommend	d. relevant
_____	5. a. accumulate	b. accelerate	c. accomodate	d. concurred
_____	6. a. judgment	b. concensus	c. excusable	d. caress
_____	7. a. sheriff	b. vilify	c. batallion	d. harass
_____	8. a. villain	b. skilfull	c. embarrass	d. relevance
_____	9. a. questionnaire	b. religious	c. sacreligious	d. tobacco
_____	10. a. withold	b. banana	c. superintendent	d. insistent
_____	11. a. wield	b. weird	c. preceed	d. proceed
_____	12. a. separate	b. desparate	c. legitimate	d. likable
_____	13. a. apalling	b. perceive	c. maneuver	d. persistent
_____	14. a. loneliness	b. misstate	c. resistent	d. accessible
_____	15. a. theater	b. massacre	c. fierce	d. hygeine
_____	16. a. credible	b. caffeine	c. dilemma	d. divisable
_____	17. a. seige	b. leisure	c. weird	d. fierce
_____	18. a. calendar	b. gaiety	c. collossal	d. playwright
_____	19. a. rhythm	b. sergeant	c. wintry	d. suprise
_____	20. a. successful	b. embarrasses	c. harrassed	d. impressive
_____	21. a. category	b. comparative	c. omitted	d. useable
_____	22. a. wholly	b. desirable	c. changeable	d. noticeable
_____	23. a. missile	b. admireable	c. mileage	d. reign
_____	24. a. assassin	b. benefitted	c. mortgage	d. miniature
_____	25. a. discrete	b. interment	c. exagerrate	d. phenomena

EXERCISE 33

Spelling 3

Purpose: To continue to seek mastery of spelling.

Reference: *WWC* (4/e), Chapter 8; your dictionary

Instructions: In each of the following sentences, one or more words may be spelled incorrectly. When you find an incorrectly spelled word, cross it out and write in the proper spelling. (In some sentences all words are spelled correctly.)

1. Her attornies introduced documents coroborating the charge of sexual harassment.

2. Conditions in the convalesent home were indescribable.

3. Although suseptible to occasional siezures of sloth, he is a suprisingly efficient worker.

4. The personable sophomore succumbed to skepticism.

5. The latest reconnissance mission yielded much relevent information about enemy forces.

6. His prounciation of certain words was noticably plebian.

7. The stationary was beautifully imbossed, but unfortunately the address was illegible.

8. He wanted to excell as a superviser, but the workers thought of him as a numskull.

9. Her favorite pastime was correcting mispellings on posted notices.

10. The misellaneous merchandize includes twelve tins of tobbaco and forteen reversable jackets.

11. His predecessor, the sargent, had an outrageous temper.

12. Daily excercise is exhillarating, according to legions of amateur athletes.

13. The superintendant, known for her perserverance, had an irrepressible sense of humor.

14. He said the homemade mayonaise was completely indigestable.

15. The bookkeeper was besieged by a formidable arry of tax auditors.

16. Your superviser has occassionally been wrong, but you should yield to his judgement in most cases.

17. His persistence and irresistible logic finally persuaded the superintendent.

18. His predecessor always asked for separate checks.

19. The bookeeper alledgedly omitted all of his personal expense account reports from the audit.

20. It's my privelege not to reccommend this special procedure.

EXERCISE 34

Spelling 4

Purpose: To continue to improve spelling mastery through a focus on the editing process.

Reference: *WWC* (4/e), Chapter 8; your dictionary

Instructions: Please review the following paragraphs and correct all spelling errors. (There are 25.)

In a turse memmorandum to the Plainview City Council, the bond firm of Wheatley and Sims announced today that it could not reccommend the upgradding of the city's bond rating to an "AA" level.

"This is going to wreck havoc on our plans to float a bond issue for the new convention center," said City Manager Sara Smith. "Frankly, I'm embarassed."

In explaining its decision, the bond firm said there is little liklihood that the city could put forth any further arguement for the upgrade. The report concluded: "So many of its public works projects have accummulated serious indebtedness that the city is simply not a credable risk at this point."

Preceeding that anouncement, the council learned that federal funding for a sewer project had been witheld because of an ongoing dispute with federal officials over a citizen complaint about lack of accessability to city hall by people with disabilities.

"This hasn't been our day," admited Mayor Frank Thomas. "In my judgement, we are putting ourselves in jeapordy by not havin a legitamate plan of action to solve these problems."

City councilor Theresa Hart was more direct. "We simply don't have a committment to financial integraty here," she argued. "We can stay here all day and villify bond merchants and bureaucrats, but that won't solve this dillema."

Before ajourning the session, the council agreed to submit a three-page questionaire to several other bond firms to help asess the city's current financial standing.

EXERCISE 35

Editing for Grammar, Spelling and Style 1

Purpose: To incorporate all *WWC* readings and workbook exercises into a comprehensive editing exercise that tests grammatical principles.

Reference: *WWC* (4/e) (all); your dictionary

Instructions: Review the following sentences and correct all errors in grammar, word use, AP style and spelling. Edit on this sheet. Look carefully!

1. What the eyes see excite the brain.

2. What affect do you think this exam will have on we students?

3. Prof. William Jones inferred in his speech that supply-side economics will go the way of dinosoars.

4. The Porsche maneuvers quicker then the Lotus, it's torque-to-weight ratio is also more superior.

5. As I walked in to the police station I learned that a diner had robbed a fast food restaurant last night, because several persons at the establishment apparantly offended him.

6. Compared to the three luxury yachts moared near-by the thirty-four- ft. sailboat look like it was a prize in a Cracker Jacks box.

7. 37-year-old Janet Springs died instantly this morning when the car which she was driving collided with a telephone poll.

8. The Jayhawk offense have proven they are a unit to reckon with; especially with their new use of Tom Clarke, who they stationed in a slot.

9. The condition of these buildings are disgraceful, nevertheless they shouldn't effect our ability to hold classes their.

10. The City Counsel will not hold it's regular monthly meeting, due to a power failure which hit the City Hall complex at five o'clock.

11. Whom did he say received the Congressional appointment?

12. If I was President of the United States, I'd be happy to solve this dillema, however, I'm not, and I just cant accomodate you. None of your arguments is going to convince me to change my mind.

13. The stockbrokers that signed the anti-trust petition discovered that there employment contracts for next year have been cancelled.

14. You seem awfully anxious to try and compare me with a king of the beach male sea lion. Tell me: do I really seem that territorial?

15. Since its apparent that the dockworkers are going to honor there committment not to cross the picket line, over twelve million board feet of lumber are going to stay on those ships.

16. The young coach feels badly that her highly-touted forward has not been setting the world on fire.

17. She has entitled her new work "Smart Like Me;" however, she says she's recieving considerable resistence from her publisher about it.

18. For the fifteenth time!, I didn't rob those stock certificates.

19. Newt's new hit single lacks that exhilirating star quality punch.

20. Inflation is one of many evils which tends to perpetuate itself. For example midwestern farmers can't cope with fifteen per cent interest rates and those rates are fueled by banks attempts to attract new savers.

EXERCISE 36

Editing for Grammar, Spelling and Style 2

Purpose: To continue comprehensive editing practice.

Reference: *WWC* (4/e) (all); your dictionary

Instructions: Review the following sentences and correct all errors in grammar, word use, AP style and spelling. Look closely and read carefully!

1. Since I disagree with her in principal, I won't try and convince her that her project can't be salvaged.

2. Due to child resistent caps on pill containers childrens' deaths from aspirin overdose has been reduced by over 80%.

3. The Justice Department contends that it's anti-drug efforts have had profound affects in the inner-city.

4. The wizard dumbfounded we children with his tales of adventure and lonliness.

5. Grammar is one of those subjects which irritates her constantly.

6. Thomas Jones who lives at 2944 Baker Street is the man who police suspect of the warehouse robbery, however, his whereabouts are unknown.

7. In my judgement, everyone should consider their finances before proceding with this investment scheme.

8. The council feels badly that they can't honor their committment to award you the advertizing contract.

9. The superintendant refused to talk with the media today, however he has promised to hold a press conference tomorrow.

10. 60 tons of wheat have been shipped to the famine area.

11. The lightening which hit several of the trailer homes' was responsible also for 4 deaths in the Tampa area.

12. Governor Locey Pfeifer's name was mispelled on her official stationary.

13. None of these cigarette brands are superior to low-tar M. P. ZEMA, in fact "Zema" is the most unique tobbaco product which I have ever encountered.

14. Worried that passage would lead to a rash of lawsuits, the loitering ordinance was defeated by the council, 6-0.

15. The radio broadcaster always opened his show by saying "They'res good news tonight"!

EXERCISE 37

Clarity and Conciseness

Purpose: To use grammatical and style skills to construct clear and concise sentences.

Reference: *WWC* (4/e), Chapter 9

Instructions: Without altering their meaning, please rewrite the following sentences—paying attention to unnecessary words and phrases, to awkward sentence construction, to problems with parallelism or to anything else that detracts from clear, concise expression. Be as straightforward as you can.

Example:

It is a fact that the council meeting will be presided over by the mayor, whose name is John Lively.

Solution:

Mayor John Lively will preside over the council meeting.
(Active voice improves clarity here.)

1. Police theorized that she was the victim of murder—of a fatal strangulation.

   _____

2. I really believe, despite the fact that I remain hopeful that I am proved wrong, that the jury will not fully comprehend the strategy of the attorney for the defense.

   _____

   _____

3. The consensus of opinion of the instructors was as follows: that to pass the test, a very solid background in Greek was needed.

   _____

   _____

4. Being surrounded by thirty journalists who are all famous and who all have won national awards, can really make a person feel quite humble.

   _____

   _____

5. Journalists who don't pay attention to detail, people who work as reporters and who do not prepare very well for interviews, and the kind of reporter that can't seem to get a story turned in on time when it's due are just the type of reporters that Barbara Wexler, the "Post" managing editor, really doesn't like too much.

_____

_____

_____

_____

6. Buying and restoring old antique furniture is a hobby that Arthur Martison really loves, and now it has become the way that he makes his true living.

_____

_____

7. He won the award, which is very prestigious, on account of the fact that his photograph was the most unique.

_____

_____

8. Seeing as how a fatal accident caused the untimely death of two truck drivers, new warning signs in regards to the dangerous S curve are being installed by the highway crew.

_____

_____

9. Despite the fact that at this point in time that there is no reason why the senator should announce her plans, she went ahead and called a press conference anyway.

_____

_____

10. What the agency is attempting to do is to get people to work on the parking problem themselves.

_____

_____

11. Referring back to the original document, he repeated again his previous statement in which he said how concerned he was that his wording was not clear.

_____

_____

12. Wondering when interest rates on mortgage loans will return to 7 percent is a real concern on the part of those people in the Northwest who make their living off of the timber industry.

_____

_____

_____

EXERCISE 38

Boiling 1

Purpose: To eliminate wordiness and redundancy by editing a passage for maximum clarity.

Reference: *WWC* (4/e) (all)

Instructions: Review the following account and rewrite it into a coherent story, *half as long as the original*. Put facts in a cohesive order, without losing any essentials.

After he lost control of his late-model automobile when a butterfly flew into his face, Thomas Fitzpatrick, who is 38 years old and who lives at 2467 Tokay Lane, crashed into a large plate glass window of a Middletown supermarket this afternoon at about noon and completely destroyed two cash register stands, 35 grocery carts and a giant display of insect repellent spray cans.

Fitzpatrick, a plumber who works for the Chase Co., reportedly was not hurt, according to the police officers at the scene. But there was substantial damage to the E-Z Shop Market, which is located at 428 Hoover Avenue. Market manager Joe Albertson said he estimated the damage at around $30,000 after he made a preliminary estimate.

Fitzpatrick's car, a 1985 Audi Turbo, was totally demolished beyond repair. However, no supermarket patrons were injured, according to police reports.

In another accident across town, police reported today that Helen Demming's Corvette Stingray automobile hit a fire hydrant after she lost control of the vehicle. No one was injured, however, according to eyewitnesses.

Demming said that she took her hands from the steering wheel of the car (she was driving at the time) when she tried to slap at ants that were crawling around her ankles. The insects were "big and red," she said.

"I was really startled," said Demming. "You don't expect to find giant red ants in your car." The incident happened at 11 a.m. this morning. "The next thing I knew, my car smashed into this fire hydrant," said Demming, owner of the real estate brokerage of Demming & Walsh Co. "I guess I lost control."

Police said her car received only slight damage but that several businesses in the 400 block of Madison Ave. in Middletown (where the accident occurred) suffered flooding damage to their basements when storm sewers overflowed from the hydrant runoff. A damage estimate is not complete.

Demming is 29 years old. She lives at 1234 Burgundy Street. The crash happened at the corner of Madison and Polk Avenues.

(337 words)

EXERCISE 39

Boiling 2

Purpose: To continue your editing practice on a passage that is wordy and redundant.

Reference: *WWC* (4/e) (all)

Instructions: Review the following account and rewrite it into a coherent story, *half as long as the original*. Put the facts in a cohesive order, without losing any essentials.

What might have been nothing more than a minor traffic accident last night turned into an unfortunate tragedy when an out-of-control car sped into a group of people huddled at a bus stop and sent four women crashing through a plate glass window at 201 Cleveland Street.

Two of the women in the accident were killed, and another was critically injured with broken and severely cut legs. A fourth woman is at Municipal Hospital and is in satisfactory condition. There were no other injuries, according to police.

Police officers and witnesses said the accident occurred when a bright yellow car heading east on Cleveland Street struck the left side of a black convertible heading west on the same street. According to various reports, the yellow car went out of control and sped toward a group of 10 people waiting at a bus stop in front of Faunce Drug Store at 201 Cleveland. The car was halted by a 3-foot brick wall below the store window—but not until four women were struck by the car and were hurled through a large section of plate glass.

One of the victims, whose legs were almost severed, was pronounced dead on arrival at University Hospital. An investigation revealed that she was Alpha Bates, 78, of 311 McKinley St.

A second woman, a 75-year-old widow named Emma Smith of 235 Waubesa Avenue, died at Municipal Hospital 40 minutes after the tragic crash. A hospital representative said the woman's legs had been severed at the knees.

Next of kin have been notified in both deaths.

The injured women were reported to be 48-year-old Thelma Jones, who lives at 974 McClean Street, and Betty Chafee, who is 27 years old, of San Francisco. Jones is listed in critical condition. Chafee is listed in satisfactory condition. Both women are in Municipal Hospital.

Police continue to investigate the accident. The driver of the car that struck the women apparently escaped from the scene, and police are following up on leads to track down the suspect.

Funeral arrangements are pending.

(345 words)

EXERCISE 40

Final Grammar, Spelling and Word-Use Exam

Purpose: To evaluate your performance and progress with a comprehensive examination of grammatical principles.

PARTS OF SPEECH

Instructions: Identify the *underlined* part of speech.

_____ 1. Sheldon feels <u>bad</u> about the broken window.
    a. adverb
    b. adjective
    c. pronoun
    d. gerund

_____ 2. It looks <u>as if</u> it's going to rain.
    a. preposition
    b. adverb
    c. conjunction
    d. participle

_____ 3. She will head the <u>specially</u> commissioned panel.
    a. adverb
    b. adjective
    c. noun
    d. verb

_____ 4. <u>Between</u> you and me, these ticket prices are getting out of hand.
    a. conjunction
    b. preposition
    c. adverb
    d. verb

_____ 5. <u>lifting</u> weights can give you more flexibility than you think.
    a. noun
    b. adverb
    c. verb
    d. adjective

IDENTIFICATION OF SENTENCE ELEMENTS ,

Instructions: Identify the *underlined* sentence element.

_____ 6. Do you really believe that <u>the sun will come out tomorrow</u>?
    a. independent clause
    b. dependent (subordinate) clause
    c. adverbial clause
    d. appositive phrase

_____ 7. <u>Running on concrete</u> isn't the best thing for one's knees.
    a. subject of sentence
    b. participial phrase
    c. introductory clause
    d. predicate norminative

_____ 8. <u>After the circus left town</u>, I realized I had spent my life's savings on the water balloon game.
    a. prepositional phrase
    b. independent clause
    c. appositive clause
    d. introductory subordinate clause

_____ 9. <u>Besieged by creditors</u>, the financier quickly left town.
    a. adverbial phrase
    b. participial phrase
    c. subordinate clause
    d. prepositional phrase

_____ 10. She decided to leave all her money <u>to the SCA</u> (Society for Creative Acronyms).
    a. appositive phrase
    b. prepositional phrase
    c. participial phrase
    d. adverbial clause

SENTENCE TYPES

Instructions: Identify each of these sentences according to its type. Use the following code: a = simple; b = compound; c = complex; d = compound-complex; e = fragment.

_____ 11. Despite the ravages of a poor economy, this is going to be a good year for us contractors.

_____ 12. I thought this plan would work out, but I guess I was wrong.

_____ 13. Hitting the brakes for all he was worth as the vehicle sped wildly down the road.

_____ 14. The snowfall has clogged all the passes, but the daily newspaper still managed to get through.

_____ 15. Harmonicas that are made of plastic don't hold a tune very well.

AGREEMENT, CASE AND PUNCTUATION

Instructions: Select the correct answer from the choices offered.

_____ 16. Beyond the horizon of an ordinary mind **(a) Is (b) are** adventure and intrigue.

_____ 17. She is one of those politicians **(a) who (b) whom** party bosses never can accept.

_____ 18. There is no better graphic designer than **(a) he (b) him**.

_____ 19. Baseball is one of those games that **(a) require (b) requires** close attention to the rules.

_____ 20. Neither the attorneys nor the contractor **(a) has (b) have** been linked to the bidding scandal.

_____ 21. The Senate won't confirm his nomination **(a) because (b), because** it doesn't feel he has the background to handle such a sensitive post.

_____ 22. This weather is the type that could really injure spring crops **(a), however, (b); however (c); however,** a warm front should move in soon.

_____ 23. The **(a) witness' (b) witness's** story did not support the plaintiff's testimony.

_____ 24. Herschel is the kind of actor **(a) who (b) whom** moviegoers love to watch.

_____ 25. This award will go to **(a) whoever (b) whomever** receives the highest score on the Scholastic Aptitude Test.

_____ 26. A number of exceptional works of fiction **(a) has (b) have** appealed on the book market recently.

_____ 27. Finding and tackling "impossible" projects **(a) has (b) have** always stimulated Sarah to new levels of accomplishment.

_____ 28. More than 70,000 tons of relief supplies **(a) has (b) have** been airlifted to Ethiopia and Somalia.

_____ 29. Police arrested the demonstrators **(a) and (b), and** took them to a high school gymnasium for fingerprinting and processing.

_____ 30. Are you going to see **(a) "Camelot?" (b) "Camelot"?**

_____ 31. Neither of the witnesses **(a) sound (b) sounds** very credible.

_____ 32. I know you're surprised, but the winnings in the Washington lottery are **(a) yours (b) your's**.

_____ 33. Your criteria for evaluating my paper **(a) is (b) are** capricious.

_____ 34. None of the witnesses **(a) has (b) have** shown up for the Jackson trial.

_____ 35. It's going to be another **(a) rainy, Oregon winter (b) rainy Oregon winter**.

SPELLING

Instructions: Pick the *correct* spelling from the choices offered in the following sentences. Enter the appropriate letter in the blank on the left or on your answer sheet.

_____ 36. The <u>wierd</u> <u>villain</u> <u>weilded</u> a <u>deplorible</u> influence over the group.
              (a)   (b)   (c)   (d)

_____ 37. Can you be <u>innoculated</u> against the <u>ravages</u> of <u>tonsilitis</u> and <u>pneumonia?</u>
                   (a)   (b)   (c)   (d)

_____ 38. The <u>playright</u> was <u>embarassed</u> that she neglected to secure a <u>copywright</u> for her
              (a)   (b)   (c)

<u>colossal</u> new production.
  (d)

_____ 39. The <u>sherriff's</u> appointment <u>calender</u> is barely <u>manageable</u>; he must learn to
            (a)   (b)   (c)

<u>withold</u> more of his time.
  (d)

_____ 40. In all <u>liklihood,</u> his was a <u>concious</u> effort to destroy the <u>concensus</u> of the <u>amiable</u>
              (a)   (b)   (c)   (d)

group.

_____ 41. What do you mean, "His <u>judgment</u> is <u>infalible</u>"? That's a <u>decietful</u> <u>arguement.</u>
                        (a)   (b)   (c)   (d)

_____ 42. The <u>physicains</u> hypothesized that massive doses of <u>caffeine</u> contributed to his
           (a)   (b)

<u>horrable</u> <u>hemorhage.</u>
  (c)   (d)

_____ 43. It's <u>presumtuous</u> of you to assume that this is a <u>plausible</u> <u>occurence.</u> It's a
       (a)   (b)   (c)

<u>deploriable</u> act.
  (d)

_____ 44. The <u>sargeant</u> ordered everyone to remain <u>stationery</u>. She said she didn't want to
       (a)   (b)

hear the <u>rustle</u> of a single piece of <u>khaki.</u>
      (c)   (d)

_____ 45. This predicament <u>stupifies</u> me. I'll need <u>perseverance</u> and <u>incorruptable</u> conduct
               (a)   (b)   (c)

to resolve this <u>dilemma.</u>
      (d)

WORD USE

Instructions: Select the correct answer from the choices offered.

_____ 46. Let's drive **(a) farther (b) further** down the road.

_____ 47. He didn't mean to **(a) imply (b) infer** in his speech that you are dishonest.

_____ 48. Mussolini's corpse **(a) hanged (b) hung** in the town square.

_____ 49. This dietary plan is **(a) composed of (b) comprised of** four nutritionally approved stages.

_____ 50. You really seem **(a) anxious (b) eager** to do this.

_____ 51. It's beginning to look **(a) as if (b) like** the grand jury will return an indictment.

_____ 52. Contract negotiations have broken down **(a) among (b) between** Smith of the American League White Sox, the National's Cubs management team and free agent Winfield.

_____ 53. **(a) Compared to (b) Compared with** last year's inflation rate, this year's increase is hardly noticeable.

_____ 54. What **(a) affect (b) effect** do you think this grading policy will have on us students?

_____ 55. The club could not approve your membership in its Royal Order of Obfuscators **(a) because (b) since** you write too clearly and logically.

IDENTIFICATION OF GRAMMATICAL ERRORS

Instructions: Read the following sentences and determine whether they contain grammatical errors. If a sentence contains an error, select the lettered item that describes the error. If the sentence is correct, select _e, no error._

_____ 56. Please buckle up your seat belts as soon as you get in the car, it's the best way to protect yourselves.
   a. _It's_ should be _its._
   b. Comma should be replaced with semicolon.
   c. _Buckle up is_ awkward and redundant.
   d. Both b and c are correct.
   e. No error.

_____ 57. The argument which I was going to pursue in my closing statement has proved itself a winner in several product liability cases.
   a. _Product liability_ should be hyphenated as a compound modifier.
   b. _Proved_ should be replaced with _proven._
   c. Subordinate clause should be set off with commas.
   d. _Which_ should be replaced with _that._
   e. No error.

_____ 58. The man whom police arrested for the crime has an airtight alibi; however, police are not willing to drop the charges.

    a. *Whom* should be replaced with *who.*

    b. Improper punctuation has created a comma splice.

    c. Error in subject-verb agreement.

    d *Whom* should be replaced with that.

    e. No error.

_____ 59. None of the stockholders are going to press for a proxy battle, but they certainly showed the board they can mount a well-organized campaign.

    a. No hyphen needed in *well-organized.*

    b. Error in subject-verb agreement.

    c. Semicolon needed before *but.*

    d. Pronoun *that* needed before *board* and *they.*

    e. No error.

_____ 60. Working with all his might to trim the mainsail, the wind abeam fought his every move; but he finally brought his craft under control.

    a. Coordinating conjunction requires only a comma before it.

    b. Dangling participial phrase.

    c. Semicolon needed after *mainsail.*

    d. Two sentences required for clarity's sake.

    e. No error.